OLD TESTAMENT GUIDES

General Editor

R.N. Whybray

DEUTERONOMY

DEUTERONOMY

R.E. Clements

Published by JSOT Press
for the Society for Old Testament Study

First published by JSOT Press 1989
Reprinted 1993

Copyright © 1989, 1993 Sheffield Academic Press

Published by JSOT Press
JSOT Press is an imprint of
Sheffield Academic Press Ltd
343 Fulwood Road
Sheffield S10 3BP
England

Typeset by Sheffield Academic Press
and
Printed on acid-free paper in Great Britain
by The Charlesworth Group
Huddersfield

British Library Cataloguing in Publication Data

A catalogue record for this book is available
from the British Library

ISSN 0264-6498
ISBN 1-85075-214-1

CONTENTS

88524

ABBREVIATIONS

ATANT	Abhandlungen zur Theologie des Alten und Neuen Testaments
BETL	Bibliotheca Ephemeridum Theologicarum Lovaniensium
BWANT	Beiträge zur Wissenschaft vom Alten und Neuen Testament
CB	Coniectanea Biblica
ET	English Translation
FRLANT	Forschungen zur Religion und Literatur des Alten und Neuen Testaments
HKAT	Handkommentar zum Alten Testament
IB	Interpreter's Bible
KHC	Kurzer Hand-Commentar zum Alten Testament
SBLDS	Society of Biblical Literature, Dissertation Series
SBT	Studies in Biblical Theology
TDOT	*Theological Dictionary of the Old Testament*, ed. G.J. Botterweck and H. Ringgren, Grand Rapids: W.B. Eerdmans, 1974 -.
ThB	Theologische Bücherei
VT	*Vetus Testamentum*
WMANT	Wissenschaftliche Monographien zum Alten und Neuen Testament

1

INTRODUCTION

T HE BOOK OF DEUTERONOMY acquired its name from the Greek *deutero-nomos* (= Second Law) through a misinterpretation of the Greek (Septuagint) translation of Deut. 17.18 which refers to a copy of the law of Moses. The title, however, is an apt description for much of what is found in the book. The central part in chs. 12-26 consists of a series of laws, many of which are elaborations of earlier laws preserved in the book of Exodus. Similarly the Ten Commandments which are set out in Deut. 5.6-21 differ only slightly in their wording from the presentation of these commandments in Exod. 20.2-17. What we find in Deuteronomy is essentially a re-giving of the laws of the covenant made with Israel on Mount Horeb. These are formulated as a speech of Moses delivered in the plains of Moab, east of the River Jordan (Deut. 1.1; 34.1). This is a farewell admonition to Israel before their entry into the land (Deut. 31.1-13).

The heart of Deuteronomy is found in the collection of laws, now contained in chs. 12-26, which are prefaced by a historical introduction in chs. 1-3 and a series of speeches of exhortation and admonition in 4-11. The laws are provided with a conclusion in the form of a miscellaneous collection of addresses and poems with a historical epilogue in chs. 27-34. The book can therefore be broadly divided between a central law-book in chs. 12-26 surrounded by a framework in 1-11 and 27-34. The former part, the law-book, appears as a recognizable whole, while the framework is less unified and bears the marks of having been drawn from a wider range of material in a series of editorial stages. Understandably this has led scholars to conclude that the original kernel of the book is to be seen in the law code, which has later been expanded by the addition of an extended introduction and conclusion. This assumption is helpful up to a point, but should only be regarded as a tentative and partial explanation of the literary structure and development of the book as a whole.

In several of its features, both of form and content, the book of Deuteronomy is one of the most distinctive in the entire Old Testament. According to Lk. 10.27, Jesus, in replying to a question from a Jewish teacher about the way to eternal life, cited the monumental words of Deut. 6.5; 'You shall love the Lord your God with all your heart, and with all your soul, and with all your strength, and with all your mind; and your neighbour as yourself'. In this way the demand from the book of Deuteronomy is made into the most central of all the demands of the Old Testament, and has then been combined with a much shorter admonition from Lev. 19.18.

This quotation from Deuteronomy highlights a distinctive feature of the thought-world of the book and serves to show why it has come to be recognized as a document of outstanding importance in the Bible, and for the Jewish and Christian traditions that have been built upon it. This distinctiveness resides in the startling inwardness and psychological realism of the religious life as seen by the Deuteronomic writers. It is not simply the intense moral earnestness of the laws as evidence of a developing legal tradition in ancient Israel that explains this lasting significance, but the whole tenor of the book's spirituality. It makes its appeal to every Israelite to respond wholeheartedly to God's gracious calling of the nation by displaying a loving obedience towards him. Consequently the laws are backed up by admonitions to learn, teach, remember and obey them as the indispensable basis for the fulfilment of God's purpose on earth.

However, if we are to give a fair impression of the book of Deuteronomy as a whole, we must set alongside this strong emphasis upon loving God the sharp and bitterly uncompromising demand that it makes for the total, and merciless, destruction of the previous inhabitants of the land of Canaan. Deut. 7.2 contains the most forthright demand for racial genocide that is to be found anywhere in the Old Testament, and this too has become a distinctive feature of the book's teaching: 'And when the Lord your God gives them (the previous inhabitants of the land) over to you, and you defeat them; then you must utterly destroy them; you shall make no covenant with them, and show no mercy to them'. We thus find in Deuteronomy some of the most perceptive and uplifting, as well as the most frightful and alarming, features of the Old Testament's ethical teaching.

The book's distinctive emphasis upon right thinking about God and right feeling towards him is matched by a very carefully thought-through theology. This has given rise to an easily recognizable circle of ideas and favoured vocabulary. So marked is this that both the style and distinctive vocabulary of Deuteronomy constitute the most easily recognizable of all the distinctive theological traditions that are to be found in the Old Testament. The authors of Deuteronomy have left their stamp on the Pentateuch as a whole, and quite extensively also upon other parts of the Old Testament.

A significant moment in the rise of modern critical Old Testament Scholarship was the publication in 1805 of a thesis by the German scholar W.M.L. de Wette concerning Deuteronomy. In this he suggested that the law book which is reported in 2 Kgs 22-23 as having been found in the temple at Jerusalem was the book of Deuteronomy. Although this connection of Deuteronomy with the law book of Josiah's reform can now be seen by scholars in a rather different light from that seen by de Wette, the issue has nonetheless provided an important step towards an understanding of the literary history of the Pentateuch. Because the style of Deuteronomy is so distinctive, and because the book occupies a kind of middle point in the literary growth of the Pentateuch, its connection with the late seventh century BC, when Josiah's reform took place, provided a foundation stone for Pentateuchal criticism. In terms of literary history much that is to be found in the Pentateuch can be classed as either 'pre-', or 'post'-Deuteronomic.

In line with this recognition there are particular developments in the history of Israelite worship and theology which can similarly be identified as belonging either to an earlier, or later, stage of growth than that presented in the book of Deuteronomy.

A further feature also serves to show why this book occupies such a central position in the literary and theological study of the Old Testament. The historical books of Joshua, Judges, 1 & 2 Samuel and 1 & 2 Kings, taken as a single continuous whole, have come to be referred to as 'The Deuteronomistic History' (see R.P. Gordon, *1 & 2 Samuel*, Old Testament Guides, pp. 14-22). This is due to the fact that these books present the history of Israel from its beginnings to the end of the monarchy with the perspective that the divine law had been revealed through Moses and had been made accessible to the nation in a book. This book of the law can be seen to be identfied with the book of Deuteronomy, although probably not exactly in the form in which it now exists. In fact the introductory chapters of Deuteronomy (Deut. 1–3) are widely taken to have been intended to serve as an introduction to this work combining the law book (Deuteronomy) followed by the account of Israel's rise and fall as a nation (that is, the Deuteronomistic History). This history is, thus, an account of how Israel lived out its existence in the land promised to its ancestors in the light of the law given through Moses.

In summing up this short presentation of the significance of Deuteronomy for Old Testament study we may draw attention to a major point concerning the nature of this literature as a whole. Understandably and appropriately it focusses its attention upon the great religious figures that emerged during Israel's history: Abraham, Moses, Joshua, David and so on. Greatest of all among these figures of the Old Testament is Moses, and it is certainly the book of Deuteronomy which serves to present Moses in this perspective. The fact that Moses is the person who dominates the Old Testament above all other human figures is due in great part to the emphasis which Deuteronomy places upon him and his role in Israel's religious origins.

At the same time we must be aware that the work and achievements of all these great figures have been communicated to us through writings whose authors we do not directly know. We can only infer what were their aims and interests from what they have left to us in their books. So distinctive is the book of Deuteronomy that its authors, whom we have become accustomed to refer to simply as 'the Deuteronomists', show themselves to have been the most influential of all such groups of writers in the Old Testament. Anonymous as they must remain, they contributed extensively and in a fundamental way to the compilation of the Old Testament as a sacred literature. From a religious and spiritual perspective they show themselves to have been aware of the power and vitality of the written word. They viewed the possession of a sacred book of divine instruction as one of the greatest of God's gifts to Israel. This book was to be kept in the most holy of all places beside the very ark of the covenant (Deut. 31.9-13). Even the king was to govern his own life and that of his kingdom by reading and meditating upon it constantly (Deut. 17.18-20; cf. 1.Kgs.2.1-4). The book of Deuteronomy therefore provides us with important insights into understanding why both Judaism and Christianity have found their faith to be focussed upon a literature of sacred writings. They are both religions of a book, and it is Deuteronomy which most distinctively established the pattern for such a book-oriented spirituality.

A Note about Commentaries

Deuteronomy has been the subject of several excellent commentaries in recent years of which the most notable for English readers are those by G. von Rad and A.D.H. Mayes. The work of von Rad, *Deuteronomy, A Commentary*, (London: SCM, 1966); ET by D. Barton is a translation from *Das fünfte Buch Mose: Deuteronomium* (ATD 8; Göttingen, 1964). It summarizes, albeit rather briefly, the conclusions of two earlier studies by the same author on central issues in the book. The volume by A.D.H. Mayes, *Deuteronomy* (New Century Bible; Marshall-Pickering, London: 1979) should certainly be looked upon as the best, and most up to date, that is currently available for English language readers. The near-contemporary work by P.C. Craigie, *The Book of Deuteronomy* (New International Commentary on the Old Testament; Grand Rapids: Eerdman's 1976) is helpful, and contains much important material, but is too heavily affected by certain literary theories regarding structure and date to be a useful all round guide to recent work. Several shorter commentaries can be recommended and deserve mention, notably A. Phillips, *Deuteronomy* (Cambridge Bible Commentaries on the New English Bible; Cambridge: Cambridge University Press, 1973) and G. Ernest Wright, 'Deuteronomy', *The Interpreter's Bible* (Nashville: Abingdon, 1953). Vol. II, pp. 307-537. Cf. also J.A. Thompson, *Deuteronomy* (Tyndale Old Testament Commentaries; London Tyndale, 1974). More recently, the volume by Richard Clifford, *Deuteronomy*, (Old Testament Message, 4; Wilmington: Michael Glazier, 1982) has appeared and covers several significant issues in recent scholarly discussion.

Among older writings, the following have proved to be of lasting value and remain important for a careful study of the book: S.R. Driver, *Deuteronomy* (ICC; Edinburgh, T. & T. Clark, 3rd edn 1902) and G.A. Smith, *Deuteronomy* (Cambridge Bible for Schools and Colleges; Cambridge: Cambridge University Press, 1918). Of the older commentaries in German, the following are still well worth consulting: A Bertholet, *Deuteronomium* (KHAT; Tübingen, 1899) and C. Steuernagel, *Das Deuteronomium* (HAT; Göttingen: Vandenhoeck & Ruprecht, 1923).

Besides commentaries, two major volumes have appeared which deal extensively with major critical and theological issues concerning Deuteronomy. The first of these by M. Weinfeld, (*Deuteronomy and the Deuteronomic School* (London: OUP 1972), re-examines the range of issues touching the provenance of the book. The collection of essays edited by N. Lohfink, *Das Deuteronomium. Entstehung, Gestalt und Botschaft* (BETL 68; Leuven; Peeters, 1985), includes contributions by many of the leading experts in the field.

2

THE FORM
AND STRUCTURE
OF THE BOOK

D EUTERONOMY IS THE final book of the Pentateuch and, as such, fully lives up to its name as a 'second' law; it reiterates, in a somewhat revised form, laws which Moses had given earlier to Israel at Mount Horeb (=Sinai; Exod. 19-24). The book is formulated as a speech put into the mouth of Moses and delivered to all Israel on the eve of its entry into the land of Canaan. It can readily be divided into two major blocks of material—a central law code in 12.1–26.15, and a surrounding framework, an Introduction in 1.1–11.32 and an Epilogue in 26.16–34.12. although far from being entirely uniform and consistent in its style and presentation, the law code is much more of a coherent whole than are either the Introduction or Epilogue, where much more diverse types of address appear. The whole book, however, maintains its primary form as a speech given by Moses to Israel when they were all set to embark upon the great adventure of setting foot in the land promised to their ancestors.

1. The Four Headings

The reader of the book of Deuteronomy will be immediately struck by the fact that the book contains more than one introductory heading. Altogether there are four major superscriptions which describe the contents that follow. The first of these is located at 1.1: 'These are the words that Moses spoke to all Israel beyond the Jordan in the wilderness . . . ' It establishes that what follows is in the form of a speech of Moses delivered to 'all Israel'.

The second major heading occurs in 4.44-49 'This is the law which Moses set before the people of Israel; these are the testimonies, the statutes, and the ordinances, which Moses spoke to the people of

Israel when they came out of Egypt. . . ' A third heading is then to be found in 29.1, which presents the setting of the laws in a rather different fashion: 'These are the words of the covenant which Yahweh commanded Moses to make with the people of Israel in the land of Moab, besides the covenant which he had made with them at Horeb'. Yet a fourth heading introduces the final section of the book at 33.1: 'This is the blessing with which Moses the man of God blessed the people of Israel before his death'.

These four headings lend an overall structure to the book and have clearly been intended to do so. Even if we accept, as some scholars have done, that they derive from different times and stages in the book's composition, it would seem clear that they are now set as indicators of the different sections and units which belong to it as a whole. They do, in fact, mark out major sections of the book.

In addition there are a number of sub-headings; and we can also discern several marked differences in the kinds of material to be found in the different parts of the book. We can begin an examination of the form and structure of the book by setting out the following brief outline of its contents:

1.1–4.43	Historical Prologue in the Form of Moses' Memoirs
4.44–11.32	Exhortations Explaining the Place and Significance of the law
12.1–26.15	The Central Law Code
26.16–28.68	Further Admonitions and Warnings
29.1–32.52	The Covenant in the Plains of Moab
33.1–34.12	Moses' Farewell Blessing and Death

2. The Composition of the Book

When we examine closely the different parts of the book, we find clear evidence that a number of older sources have been used in its composition. Most prominent here is the use in the central law code of material and laws drawn from the earlier law code known as the Book of the Covenant (Exod. 20.22–23.19). The latter was undoubtedly the oldest and most comprehensive example of what we might describe as a civil law code in ancient Israel. When exactly it was composed has been a matter of debate among scholars, and opinions have been divided as to whether it originated before the introduction of the monarchy in Israel and was intended as a manual for the guidance of the tribal amphictyony (so M. Noth; cf. *Exodus. A Commentary*, ET, J.S. Bowden, London, 1962, pp. 169-94) or whether it emerged later. In the latter case it may have come under the sponsorship of the royal court, which certainly claimed authority to administer justice.

Alongside the Deuteronomic development of laws in the Book of the Covenant, there are also in Deuteronomy clear elaborations of the cultic calendar which appears with only minor differences in earlier texts in Exod. 23.1-17 (already incorporated into the Book of the Covenant) and Exod. 34.18-20. It is an important feature of the overall structure of Deuteronomy that it deals with matters relating to the legal administration of justice alongside, and closely interlocking with, matters concerning the observance of rites and duties of worship. Religion and law have become inextricably intertwined.

In many respects it is the presence in Deuteronomy of indications that it was composed with the aid of the Book of the Covenant as a source document that points to the conclusion that it also originated as a law code of a comparable nature. It has, however, subsequently been expanded to become much more than this. Many of its most enduring features are to be found in those aspects of its teaching which show a deep recognition that law, if it is simply embodied in a written code, cannot by itself change the attitudes and practices of a society. It must be thought about, reflected upon and respected in such a way that its fundamental aims and intentions are achieved.

It is in this connection that attention has been drawn to the Ten Commandments (Deut. 5.6-21) which repeat, with only minor differences, the commandments set out in Exod. 20.2-17. Earlier scholars (most notably S.R. Driver and G. Adam Smith in their respective commentaries) took the view that the Deuteronomic version of these commandments had drawn upon the earlier Exodus text as a source. More recently, however, there has emerged a growing awareness among scholars that their inclusion as the central part of the Sinai revelation was, from a literary point of view, made rather late. This suggests that the Deuteronomic version is the older of the two. Nevertheless, the nature of such a concise listing of ten fundamental demands of religion and morality, combined with their distinctive form, shows that these must once have formed an independent list. They can therefore be regarded as an independent source on which the Deuteronomic authors drew.

Our general outline of the contents of Deuteronomy has shown that the first three chapters of the book are historical in form, and are set out as a memoir addressed by Moses to the people. The historical information contained in this memoir has undoubtedly been drawn

from an older narrative text concerning the adventures of the
Israelites after they left Mount Horeb (Sinai) and journeyed through
the desert. Such a narrative source must be part of our present
Pentateuchal material and can, in fact, be identified with what we
still find in parts of the books of Exodus and Numbers. It is this
material which has been ascribed in the traditional documentary
source criticism of the Pentateuch to the J and E documents,
generally regarded by scholars as already combined into a single JE
narrative. (A list of the connections is conveniently set out in S.R.
Driver's commentary, pp. xiv-xix.) It is not necessary at this point to
consider ways in which modern criticism of the Pentateuch has
displayed much less certainty in delimiting the scope of particular
source documents. Nevertheless the summary of historical events
given in Deut. 1-3 is sufficiently related to narratives contained in
Exodus–Numbers for us to conclude that the authors of Deuteronomy
had before them older documentary source material. This recounted
the story of Israel's adventures after their escape from Egypt.

In addition to this use of sources drawn from earlier collections of
laws and from a historical narrative of Israel's origins out of Egypt,
there are other parts of the book of Deuteronomy which must once
have had an earlier independent existence. Among such we must
include the Twelve Curses of Deut. 27.15-28, which would appear to
have been at one time a fixed, and regularly recited, collection of
ritual curses uttered by the Levites. Such a list would have been
preserved within the circles of the Levites (cf. Deut. 27.14), and is
not the only part of the book of Deuteronomy to point to such a close
link with levitical groups. We should certainly conclude that the two
long poems in Deut. 32.1-43 and 33.2-29 also existed quite separately
at one time. Both would appear to be of very early date, possibly
originating at a time before the introduction of the monarchy.

Taken together, all these indications that the Deuteronomic
authors have drawn upon earlier sources for much of their material
lead to the conclusion that they recognized such older material to be
fundamental to Israel's knowledge of God, and that they eagerly
desired to uphold and preserve such traditions. However, the
Deuteronomic authors were certainly not mere collectors, nor were
they traditionalists in any narrowly conceived sense. What they have
given us in their book is a highly original and fresh composition; and
it is this originality and freshness that mark its great importance for
the emergence of the Old Testament.

We are entitled to draw the conclusion that the task of revising the laws of the Book of the Covenant and the composition and compilation of the book of Deuteronomy was one undertaken by a specific circle of authors. That they were more than a single author is indicated by considerable divergence of structure, style and presentation which point unmistakably to this conclusion. At the same time there is a coherence and uniformity of purpose evident throughout the book sufficient to show that it cannot have been the work of a purely miscellaneous body of writers.

At one time a number of scholars took the view that Deuteronomy had been put together from a number of separate source documents, traces of which might still be identified in the extant book. This, however, is a position which we must now set aside as implausible in itself and unnecessary in view of the evidence to be found in the book itself. Rather, an original law book has been built up, and progressively supplemented and expanded, so that it has taken on, in its final form, a rather different appearance from that which it originally took. In spite of its containing so much legal material and having as its centre a code of laws, it is now more a book of instruction concerning the nature of Israel and its unique obligations as the people of God, than a law book in the narrower legal sense. As it has grown in size and scope, so also has it been greatly modified and extended in its range and purpose.

In an essay on the overall form and character of the Book of Deuteronomy, S. Dean McBride has canvassed the idea that it can best be described as a book of 'polity' (cf. the Greek *politeia*) concerning the identity and constitution of Israel (S. Dean McBride, 'Polity of the Covenant People', *Interpretation* 41, 1987, pp. 229-44). This article certainly draws attention to many aspects of the book which are not properly described in the conventional term 'law'. However, valuable though the notion of polity is for some features, it fails to give adequate attention to the striking passages where Deuteronomy urges a very personal and individual life-style and spirituality. In some of its aspects Deuteronomy is esentially a book of 'education', and this accords with its own claim that the teaching within should be a fundamental basis for the life and daily routine of an Israelite's home (cf. Deut. 6.6-9). The authors of Deuteronomy have described their book as one of *torah* (=instruction); it is difficult to find any one English word which combines the many aspects of what this term conveys and what this book contains. To call it a book

of law is certainly to define its contents far too narrowly, even though
the revision of an earlier law code still forms its central core.

3. The Literary Forms of the Book

We have pointed out that the book of Deuteronomy as a whole is
formulated as a speech of Moses addressed to all Israel. It is
appropriate therefore that the individual laws and cultic rules that
are set out should maintain this form and should address the people
as though Moses himself were actually speaking to them. This is
already the case with the earlier Book of the Covenant. However,
laws need to be couched in forms of words appropriate to their
function. A. Alt, in a celebrated essay ('The Origins of Israelite Law',
Essays on Old Testament History and Religion ET R.A. Wilson,
Oxford, 1966, pp. 79-132; the original German edition appeared in
1934) identified two main types, or forms, of Israelite law. These he
labelled 'apodictic' and 'casuistic', the former being presented as the
direct speech of God and the latter expressed in an impersonal, third-
person, manner. The Ten Commandments are examples of the
former type, while much of the Book of the Covenant is couched in
the latter style. Thus the older legal formulations have been retained
despite the fact that the Book of the Covenant is represented as a
speech mediated through Moses. So also in Deuteronomy the Ten
Commandments (5.6-21) are presented as the direct speech of God,
while elsewhere in the book the third person form has been
preserved.

But it is a distinctive feature of the laws of Deuteronomy that,
although the third-person legal formulations remain, they are now
presented in a very evident *preaching* style. G. von Rad summarizes
this state of affairs very clearly: 'Deuteronomy is not divine law in
codified form, but preaching about the commandments—at least, the
commandments appear in a form where they are very much
interspersed with parenesis' (G. von Rad, *Studies in Deuteronomy*,
ET, D.M.G. Stalker, London, SBT 9, 1953, p. 15; the original
German edition was published in 1948). In Deuteronomy it is the
emphasis upon how the law is to be received, understood, and acted
upon that colours the book as a whole. Therefore it is difficult to
suppose that its authors were legal administrators in the professional
sense. They are rather preachers, who have found in the law an
important instrument for guarding religious faith and public
morality. Quite apart from passages in the law code (Deut. 12.1-

26.15) where the Book of the Covenant has provided a primary source, there are other passages where older short collections appear to have been used (von Rad illustrates the point from Deut. 16.19— an examplar for judges—and Deut. 22.5-11—preservation of the sacral order (von Rad, *op. cit.*, pp. 18-19).

Von Rad explains this highly distinctive Deuteronomic type of instructional law as emanating from a regular practice of preaching about the law undertaken by levites at the major religious festivals of Israel. In particular he points to the Feast of Tabernacles (cf. Deut. 31.10) as such an occasion. Undoubtedly it is this preaching aspect of the Deuteronomic law code which provides us with a most important clue to its origin and purpose. It is not a law code in the more formal sense of a handbook of legal rulings designed for the guidance of judges. It is, rather, a popular series of instructions and exhortations concerning the role of law in society and in the service of God. F. Horst endeavoured to find a suitable analogy for a lawbook of this nature by calling it *Privilegrecht*—a law of privileges for those who stood under the protection and support of a feudal lord (F. Horst, 'Das Privilegrecht Jahwes (Rechtsgeschichtliche Untersuchungen zum Deuteronomium)', *Gottes Recht. Studien zum Recht im alten Testament*, Th B 12, Munich, 1961, pp. 17-154; the original German edition appeared in 1930). Helpful as this analogy is in drawing attention to what is so unusual in Deuteronomy, it nonetheless provides us only with a partial comparison. It is in any case necessary to keep in mind that the homiletical features of the law code in Deuteronomy are carried still further in the hortatory speeches of Deut. 4-11. Similarly the series of blessings and curses in chs. 28-30 are a development related to the admonitory purpose which the other parts of the book display.

Overall we can simply note two main points. Just as Deuteronomy bears all the signs of having been composed, not at a single stroke, but over a period of time, so also does it contain materials of different types of law and cultic regulation, emanating from different sources and areas of life. These have been integrated by the Deuteronomistic authors into a coherent book by the application throughout of a passionately expressed homiletical purpose. To call Deuteronomy a lawbook in the conventional sense could therefore lead to a serious misrepresentation of its contents. It is more in the nature of a collection of homilies and sermons in which established laws form the basic texts.

4. **Deuteronomy as a Covenant Document**

In Deut. 5.2 the encounter between Israel and God on Mount Horeb
during which the Ten Commandments were revealed is described as
a 'covenant' (Heb. *berith*). Then later, in the Epilogue to the law code
at Deut. 29.1, the occasion when the contents of Deuteronomy were
first revealed to Israel in the plains of Moab is described as the
promulgation of another covenant in addition to that made earlier at
Mount Horeb. Clearly this later covenant is intended to be seen as an
extension of the earlier one, rather than as an altogether new
covenant, since the first is not to be thought of as abrogated.

The introduction of the idea of covenant into the book of
Deuteronomy is undoubtedly an important development; and we
find in later writings that have been influenced by the Deuteronomistic circle that the concept of covenant has become a very
significant one. This is most evident in the account of Josiah's reform
in 2 Kgs 22–23 and in the book of Jeremiah. The special significance
that this has for the Deuteronomic understanding of the constitution
of Israel should be considered among the major theological themes of
the book (see below under ch. 5). It should be noted in addition that
the idea of a covenant relationship existing between God and Israel
has been regarded as a major factor in determining the form of the
present book.

A number of scholars have noted strikingly close parallels between
certain passages of the Old Testament in which covenant-making is
recounted and the forms of certain non-Israelite documents from the
ancient Near East (the subject is very carefully examined by D.J.
McCarthy, *Old Testament Covenant. A Survey of Current Opinions*,
Oxford: Blackwell, 1972). Several of these treaty texts, especially
those from the Hittite sphere of political influence, emanate from the
late second millennium B.C. This led M.G. Kline, among others (cf.
his *Treaty of the Great King. The Covenant Structure of Deuteronomy*,
Grand Rapids: Eerdmans; 1963), to argue that the form of Deuteronomy
is so closely modelled in the form of these treaty documents that it
must represent a direct borrowing. Furthermore Kline, followed by
P.C. Craigie (cf. his commentary on Deuteronomy) and J.G.
McConville (cf. his *Law and Theology in Deuteronomy*), argue that it
is precisely the late second millennium form of such treaties that is
followed, so that Deuteronomy itself must therefore be of second
millennium origin. This conclusion, however, cannot be sustained on
the grounds of the actual contents of the book. On grounds of method

alone it is clearly very unwise to allow similarities of form, which are susceptible to many explanations, to take precedence over major features of actual content. However, there are certainly striking similarities to be noted between the form of Deuteronomy as it now exists and the form of these ancient Near Eastern treaty documents.

We should, in the first instance, rule out the attempt of Kline, Craigie and others to define a specifically second millennium form of such treaty documents. Closely comparable texts are to be found from the Assyrian sphere in the seventh century BC, much closer in date to the book of Deuteronomy which can be ascertained on other grounds. Even though there are, as we should expect, some variations between one series of texts and others, there is a remarkable consistency in the form. This ought not to occasion surprise since it is the situations with which such treaties were designed to deal that has exercised a controlling influence on the form.

M.G. Kline (*op. cit., passim*) finds in the book of Deuteronomy the following features:

1. Preamble: Covenant Mediator, Deut. 1.1-5
2. Historical Prologue: Covenant History, Deut. 1.6-4.49
3. Stipulations: Covenant Life, Deut. 5.1-26.49
4. Sanctions: Covenant Ratification, Deut. 27.1-30.20
5. Dynastic Disposition: Covenant Continuity, Deut. 31.1-34.12.

Some of these divisions advocated by Kline do not accord with the actual literary structures of the book's own growth; nevertheless, the parallels are substantial. If we follow our primary conclusion that the book of Deuteronomy has acquired its final shape over a long period of growth, perhaps extending to as long as a century, it would appear that the assimilation to a covenant form was a part of this process. This would accord satisfactorily both with the fact that the authors of Deuteronomy can be confidently assumed to have been familiar with the diplomatic and international protocol of Assyrian rule, and also with the fact that the notion of covenant appears to have come into the book at a late stage. It would then be reasonable to suppose that the introduction of the claim that Deuteronomy is the literary deposit of a covenant made in the plains of Moab (Deut. 29.1) was followed by a structuring of Deuteronomy along the lines of a covenant, or treaty, text. The close links between the book of Deuteronomy and the form of such ancient treaty texts has been very fully explored by D.J. McCarthy, *Treaty and Covenant*, *Analecta Biblica 21A*, Rome: Biblical Institute Press, 1978. If this position is adopted, then we may conclude that the claim that the book of Deuteronomy follows the form of such ancient Near Eastern political treaties is to be upheld, but that this tells us little directly about the precise time when this assimilation to a covenant form was adopted.

Further Reading

Issues relating to the form and structure of the book have usually been dealt with in close relation to other aspects of it. However, the study by G. von Rad, *Studies in Deuteronomy* (SBT 9), London, 1953, pp. 11-24, marked an important step in the discussion. The study of covenant forms is examined in detail in D.J. McCarthy, *op.cit.*, pp. 157-205. Cf. also Klaus Baltzer, *The Covenant Formulary in Old Testament, Jewish and Early Christian Writings*, ET D.E. Green, 1971, pp. 31-38. A general survey of recent critical approaches to the book of Deuteronomy is offered in H.D. Preuss, *Deuteronomium*, Erträge der Forschung 164, Darmstadt, 1982.

3

THE CENTRAL
LAW CODE

W E HAVE SEEN THAT the heart of the book of Deuteronomy is to be found in the central law code of 12.1–26.15. This consists of a revised and up-dated form of earlier laws, chiefly drawn from the Book of the Covenant of Exod. 20.22–23.19, and partly of a range of civil laws which appear in Deuteronomy for the first time. What is most original in Deuteronomy, however, and constitutes the most striking feature of the book, is the large number of rules governing worship and prohibited practices of alien worship, which are closely integrated into the overall structure of the law code. We may present the following short outline of the main contents of the code:

I. *Laws Governing Worship*

1. 12.1-32 The Law of the Central Sanctuary
2. 13.1–14.2; 16.21–17.7; 18.9-14 The Avoidance of False Worship
3. 14.3-21 Clean and Unclean Animals
4. 14.22-29; 15.19-23 Tithes and Firstlings
5. 15.1-18 The Year of Release and the Freeing of Slaves
6. 16.1-17 The Festival Calendar

II. *Offices and Institutions*

1. 16.18-20; 17.8-13; 19.14-21 The Administration of Justice
2. 17.14-20 The Appointment of the King
3. 18.1-8 Provision for Levitical Priests
4. 18.9-22 The Role of Prophets
5. 19.1-13 The Cities of Refuge
6. 20.1-20 The Conduct of War

III. *Miscellaneous Laws*

1. 21.1-9 Unaccounted Death
2. 21.10-22.30 Marriage and Family Life
3. 23.1-25 Persons Excluded from the Community and Other Laws
4. 24.1-22 The Protection of Persons
5. 25.1-19 The Maintenance of Order and Justice
6. 26.1-15 The Offering of Firstfruits

1. *Deuteronomic Revision of Earlier Laws*

We have already noted that the law code of Deuteronomy is built upon a revision of many of the earlier laws to be found in the Book of the Covenant (Exod. 20.22-23.19). G. von Rad (*Comm.*, p. 13) lists the correspondences in the following way:

Exod. 21.1-11	=	Deut. 15.12-18
Exod. 21.12-14	=	Deut. 19.1-13
Exod. 21.16	=	Deut. 24.7
Exod. 22.16f.	=	Deut. 22.28-29
Exod. 22.21-24	=	Deut. 24.17-22
Exod. 22.25	=	Deut. 23.19-20
Exod. 22.26f.	=	Deut. 24.10-13
Exod. 22.29f.	=	Deut. 15.19-23
Exod. 22.31	=	Deut. 14.3-21
Exod. 23.1	=	Deut. 19.16-21
Exod. 23.2f., 6-8	=	Deut. 16.18-20
Exod. 23.4f.	=	Deut. 22.1-4
Exod. 23.9	=	Deut. 24.17f.
Exod. 23.10f.	=	Deut. 15.1-11
Exod. 23.12	=	Deut. 5.13-15
Exod. 23.13	=	Deut. 6.13
Exod. 23.14-17	=	Deut. 16.1-17
Exod. 23.19a	=	Deut. 26.2-10
Exod. 23.19b	=	Deut. 14.21b

This series of correspondences can be either increased or decreased depending on the degree of closeness we expect to find in the different law collections. Where the same matter is dealt with in two different law codes we should naturally expect to find a certain measure of overlap. But these correspondences go beyond this. They show that the basis of Deuteronomy is a written law code which represents a further development of the kind of law collection which we have in the Book of the Covenant, which was itself based on a legal tradition that can be traced far back in the civilization of the ancient Near East. An early written law code existed in ancient Sumer (cf. S.N. Kramer, *From the Tablets of Sumer*, Indian Hills: Falcon's Wing, 1956, pp. 47ff.), and undoubtedly the most famous is that of Hammurabi (ca. 1750 BC; cf. G.R. Driver and J.C. Miles, *The Babylonian Laws*, Oxford: OUP, 1952).

When we examine in detail the nature of this Deuteronomic revision of the earlier laws taken from the Book of the Covenant we are brought face to face with a number of interesting features of the development of Israel's legal system. It becomes clear in the first place that the Deuteronomic law is the later version and has been designed to take account of a wider range of features than those reflected in the earlier law. This becomes clear, for example, when we examine the law concerning homicide and the importance it demonstrates of the necessity for distinguishing between accidental and intentional killing. The law of the Book of the Covenant reads:

> Whoever strikes a man so that he dies shall be put to death. But if he did not lie in wait for him, but God let him fall into his hand, then I will appoint for you a place to which he may flee. But if a man willfully attacks another to kill him treacherously, you shall take him from my altar, that he may die' (Exod. 21.12-14).

When we compare this with the revised form of the law as set out in Deut. 19.1-13 we find that it has been incorporated into a larger set of provisions concerning the allocation of six cities to serve as the specified places of refuge (they are called 'cities of refuge' in Num. 35.6, 11). These are to serve as substitutes for the sanctuaries of the older law (cf. the reference to the 'altar' in Exod. 21.14). We notice that the whole question of investigation of the crime and of establishing guilt by showing a motive for murder has been dealt with more extensively. A matter of prime concern in dealing with cases of murder was the need to assess culpability. This could only be achieved by establishing some idea of motive; and this required a knowledge both of the circumstances of death and of the culprit's intentions toward the victim. From the more advanced legal system presupposed by Deuteronomy we can see that much less responsibility has been placed upon the 'avenger of blood' and upon the priests of the cultus. M. Fishbane speaks (*Biblical Interpretation in Ancient Israel*, p. 244) of an 'increasing rationalization of the juridical process'. This led to the establishment of a system of officers and judges (Deut. 16.18) who were to handle all normal legal cases. They were clearly expected to make whatever assessments they could in the light of what they could discover about the relationships between the culprit and the victim, much as a modern murder investigation would be expected to do. Only when these officers were unable to reach a satisfactory verdict was recourse to be made to the levitical priests who were to be found at the central sanctuary (Deut. 17.8-13).

One of the problems that comes to the surface in the way that Deuteronomy presupposes a revision of legal administration in ancient Israel is that there was evidently considerable difficulty for the men and women of antiquity in establishing effective laws of evidence. To accept a very limited amount of evidence as proof of guilt would leave the way open for a great many abuses. On the other hand to require overwhelming proof before making a conviction would have made it almost impossible ever to attain a verdict.

The ruling of the law of evidence in Exod. 23.1-3 runs quite tersely: 'You shall not utter a false report. You shall not join hands with a wicked man, to be a malicious witness. You shall not follow a multitude to do evil; nor shall you bear witness in a suit, turning aside after a multitude, so as to pervert justice; nor shall you be partial to a poor man in his suit' (Exod. 23.1-3). When we compare this with what we find in Deut. 19.15-21 we can see that it has been elaborated to a quite considerable degree. The revised law demands that a charge be supported by at least two, and if possible three, witnesses for it to be sustained. The Deuteronomic provision also envisages the further examination of witnesses to check on their veracity (Deut. 19.18). The new law then further lays down penalties where perjury has been committed (19.19), and this is amplified by the mention that such penalties are to serve as a deterrent. Quite clearly the need to check on witnesses, combined with the difficulty of weeding out malicious cases of collusion between unprincipled witnesses, had to be taken fully into account. In this respect we can see how the Deuteronomic legislation has become conscious of the need to resort to a principle of deterrence in its efforts to establish a rational and fair judicial system.

We can see further aspects of the way in which Deuteronomy has built upon the greater simplicity of the older Book of the Covenant when we note the way in which the later law presupposes a more advanced economic order. Ownership of property and systems of sale and exchange in the Book of the Covenant are relatively unsophisticated. They have become much more sophisticated in the Deuteronomic Code; this is reflected in the development of the law concerning the release of slaves after they have fulfilled their allotted time of servitude.

The law of Exod. 21.2f. envisages the case of a slave bought from a previous owner, who is then obligated to fulfil six years of slave service. The development of this in Deut. 15.12ff. recognizes the rather different situation of debt-slavery. In this the person concerned is considered to have sold himself into slavery in order to clear debts that have been incurred (cf. M. Fishbane, *op.cit.*, pp. 340f.). The Deuteronomic legislation also considers the possibility of women being entitled to inherit and own property in a manner which is not envisaged in the earlier code.

2. Regulations Governing Worship

We have noted earlier that there is added on to the end of the Book of the Covenant a short calendar of the major religious festivals which Israelites were bound to observe (Exod. 23.14-17). An impressive and striking feature of the Deuteronomic law code is that a more elaborate version of this festival calendar (Deut. 16.1-17) has been incorporated into the very heart of the collection. Moreover other features regarding worship, for example the law of the altar of Exod. 20.24-26, have been expanded extensively and woven fully into the Deuteronomic legislation (Deut. 12.2-14). Laws relating to religious observance have been set alongside more strictly legal matters and incorporated into a code in which both are given similar importance. The law of the central sanctuary in Deut. 12.2-14 must certainly be regarded as one of the most distinctive features of the Deuteronomic legislation. It represents a milestone of great significance in the development of worship in ancient Israel. The toleration of a wide variety of altars and sanctuaries can be described as 'pre-Deutero-nomic', whereas insistence on a single sanctuary can be recognized as belonging to a period after this Deuteronomic demand had become an established fact.

It is also significant that the manner in which most of Israel's and Judah's kings are criticised in the history of 1 & 2 Kings up to the time of Josiah's great reform (2 Kgs 22-23), demonstrates the influential outworking of this Deuteronomic legislation. Nor is it difficult to understand why Deuteronomy has sought to introduce such a restrictive rule concerning sacrificial worship which in other respects must have proved highly inconvenient (cf. 14.24-26). It is part of its endeavour to implement a widespread purification of the worship of God in Israel by removing the opportunity and occasion for retaining any vestiges of the older Canaanite worship of Baal and other gods and goddesses (12.2-3; cf. also 13.1-5, 6-11, 12-18). By restricting sacrificial worship to one single sanctuary far greater control could be exercised over its activities.

From the perspective of a forward-looking speech of Moses, delivered in Transjordan, the central sanctuary was to be identified by its possession of the ark where the tablets of law were kept (10.1-5; 31.24-29). During the age in which Deuteronomy was actually composed in the late seventh century BC there can be no doubt that this sanctuary was clearly identified as that of Jerusalem with its temple. It was the need to avoid an obvious anachronism that has led to the absence of any more specific naming. The sanctuary in question is simply referred to as the place which God himself would designate. However, a positive identification is made in the later historical writing; and clearly Jerusalem was the place around which the seventh-century centralization took place, as 2 Kgs 22-23 shows. From the Deuteronomic point of view it was important to show that there had been an unbroken continuity of worship since the time of God's revelation at Mount Horeb until the ark had been brought into Jerusalem in David's time (2 Sam. 6.12-15). It is in furtherance of such a contention that writers influenced by the Deuteronomic legislation claimed that in the time before David's conquest of Jerusalem there had been such a sanctuary at Shiloh, where the ark had been kept (1 Sam. 3.3; Jer. 7.12-15; Ps. 78.60, 67-68).

It is wholly in keeping with the Deuteronomic concern to bring together a wide range of religious and social concerns that it should include a comprehensive calendar of religious festivals (Deut. 16.1-17). This clearly represents an expansion and development from that laid down in the older shorter festival calendars preserved in Exod. 23.14-17 and 34.8-24. At the same time it is less developed than the much fuller calendar preserved in Lev. 23.1-44, showing how the Deuteronomic legislation represents a middle position in the records of Israel's developing system of worship.

What is especially noteworthy about these Deuteronomic rules for worship is the manner in which they combine into one single spring festival the celebration of the Feast of Passover (Heb, *Pesah*; Deut. 16.1-2, 5-7) with that of the Feast of Unleavened Bread (Heb. *Massot*;

Deut. 16.3-4, 8). There can be no doubt that this marks a carefully considered concern to bind together two festival celebrations which were originally separate in their origin. One of these was a shepherds' sacrificial rite, most probably occurring at the time when the flocks were moved into new pasturelands. The rites relating to the eating of unleavened bread on the other hand, were celebrated by those living off the sown land and marked the consumption of the last of the previous year's grain stocks. It would appear that because an economic situation had developed in which both patterns of agriculture had come to exist side by side, the accompanying religious rites were linked together.

Two other features relating to this spring festival deserve special attention. The first of these is that the purpose of such a celebration is very firmly laid down as an act of 'remembering' the event of the exodus from Egypt (Deut. 16.1-8). In this way the more surface aspects of the agricultural significance are left in the background. The second is the firm insistence that the Passover should be celebrated at the sanctuary which God would choose (Deut. 16.6-7), and not in the domestic settlements of the worshippers. It is probable that, by combining these spring celebrations, Deuteronomy was simply acknowledging a practice that had already become an established convention for some groups in Israel.

We ought not to leave consideration of the Deuteronomic rules for worship without noting the significance of the inclusion of the list of clean and unclean animals in Deut. 14.3-20. This is concluded by a prohibition against eating any creature that has died of its own accord (i.e., has not be slaughtered). Alongside this there is a further prohibition against boiling a kid in its mother's milk. This has long been a rule shrouded in obscurity, but must certainly have been related to some form of alien (Canaanite) religious ritual.

Deuteronomy moved very positively towards the establishment of a set of comprehensive rules concerning profane and holy things which was to have a profound effect upon Judaism. In the late post-exilic period the development of dietary laws, based on an understanding of 'clean' and 'unclean' goods, was to give rise to a distinctive body of domestic rituals and to provide Judaism with a readily identifiable charter of religious loyalty. Even within Deuteronomy we can see how a very wide area of daily life has been drawn into the sphere of the holy, in accordance with Deuteronomy's own deep assumption that it is the people of Israel who are themselves 'holy'. Deuteronomy consequently shows comparatively little concern

with the idea of holy places and objects. Undoubtedly this went hand
in hand with Deuteronomy's own conviction, that much that popular
tradition regarded as 'holy' was in fact a danger to the authentic
religious tradition of the nation.

3. Distinctive Laws in Deuteronomy

Besides developments and modifications of earlier laws and the
elaboration of regulations governing worship there are in Deuteronomy
many legal prescriptions which do not appear in earlier texts. Of
special interest among these is a series of laws relating to the conduct
of war and the obligations for military service. These cover such
issues as circumstances entitling a man to exemption from military
service (20.1-9), the conduct of an army when besieging a city (20.10-
20) and the necessity for maintaining firm hygienic discipline in a
military camp (23.9-14). All of these rules must certainly relate to
concerns and conventions that had originated far earlier than the
time of Deuteronomy and are simply being recorded here for the first
time. What is rather unexpected is their inclusion in such a law code
as this, since they deal with specifically military matters. Significantly
they record traditions and customs related to the long-established
notion of 'holy war' (cf. G. von Rad, *Studies in Deuteronomy*, pp. 45-
59).

The inclusion of these regulations governing warfare would
certainly suggest that Deuteronomy arose at a time when Israel was
facing something of a military crisis. It is also significant that such
regulations presuppose that Israel's defence was primarily a matter
for the civilian conscripted militia, rather than for a central corps of
professional soldiers, such as must have grown up as a part of Israel's
royal establishment from the time of David and Solomon.

Besides a number of miscellaneous laws which appear in Deuteronomy for the first time aimed at protecting the environment (cf.
Deut. 22.6-7) and requiring a responsible attitude towards the
building and maintenance of property (cf. Deut. 22.8), the most
striking new introduction is a law defining the position of the king
(Deut. 17.14-20). This is the only biblical statement concerning the
constitutional position of the monarch, and it contains a number of
striking features. In the first place the requirement that he should be
'one from among your brethren' (Deut. 17.15) excludes a foreigner
from such office. At the same time there is no hint that he is anything
other than an ordinary mortal human being, so that all traces of an

older divine mythology concerning the king's status are set aside. The highest that is affirmed regarding him is that he must be one whom God himself has chosen. Certainly this reflects a concept of divine election, but it gives no clear indication how this divine election was to be defined. Almost certainly we should understand it as operative through a traditional dynasty and to be a pointer to the importance attached by the Deuteronomic authors to the dynasty of David. However, this is only made clear through the historical narratives of 1 & 2 Samuel and is not defined more closely in the book of Deuteronomy itself. A further feature is very noteworthy. Since only a very skeletal outline is given here relating to the duties of the king, the emphatic stipulation that he should not amass either horses or wives (vv. 16-17) must relate to an issue that was very keenly felt. Clearly only Solomon can have been in mind in such a specification; and this points us to an aspect of popular political memory in Israel of which the Deuteronomists were very conscious. We may also note that the surprisingly pietistic demand in vv. 18-20 that the king should personally read and study the law book of Deuteronomy points to a bold claim on the part of such lawmakers that their authority was higher than that of the king. We shall see, when we come to consider the significance and meaning of the framework to the laws, that this was wholly in accord with the central role ascribed to Moses in Israel's history.

Further Reading

The law code is undoubtedly the most central feature of the book, and naturally figures prominently in most of the general introductions to the Old Testament and in general treatments of the development of Israelite worship, among others, H.H. Rowley, *Worship in Ancient Israel*, London: SPCK, 1967. As regards the development of Israel's system of law, the following two works are generally useful: H.-J. Boecker, *Law and the Administration of Justice in the Old Testament and the Ancient Near East*, ET J. Moiser, London: SPCK, 1980; Dale Patrick, *Old Testament Law*, London: SCM 1985. Special attention should also be given to the valuable sections dealing with Deuteronomy in M. Fishbane, *Biblical Interpretation in Ancient Israel*, Oxford: Oxford University Press, 1984. Some comparable treatment is also to be found in J. Weingreen, *From Bible to Mishna*, Manchester: Manchester University Press, 1976.

4

THE FRAMEWORK
TO THE LAWS

IF THE LAW CODE of 12.1–26.15 represents the central, and also, in most respects, the oldest part of the book of Deuteronomy, the framework that surrounds it, providing it with both an Introduction and an Epilogue, is nonetheless an important accessory to it. However, while the law code now bears a relatively uniform and coherent structure, the framework that surrounds it appears to be more haphazard in its arrangement and lacking in unity. The presence of separate headings in 1.1; 4.44–49; 29.1; 31.1; 31.30 and 33.1, together with a concluding eulogy of Moses in 34.10-12, shows how a formal structure has been given to the book as a whole. This structure helps to keep together the very different kinds of material which provide the contents to the framework. In general, we must conclude, as most scholars have in fact concluded, that the law code was itself built up in stages and that similar, and far more extensive, additions were made to the framework. The material is neither all of one kind, nor is it expressed through a completely unified set of theological ideas. In fact some of the most distinctive of Deuteronomy's theological ideas appear only in certain specific parts of the book. Perhaps most striking of all is the fact that, whereas the figure of Moses is largely absent from the law code, it completely dominates the framework.

1. **The Introduction and Epilogue**

We must first set out a list of the contents of the Introduction and Epilogue in order to show the differences in the kind of material that are to be found there:

A. INTRODUCTION: 1.1–11.32

B. EPILOGUE: 26.16–34.12

We can make a straightforward assessment of the different kinds of material that are to be found here: chs. 1–3 and 34 are historical narrative recalling Israel's adventures in the wilderness and then recalling the death of Moses. Chapter 31 sets out provision for the writing down of the law and its preservation. Thereafter chs. 32 and 33 are two long poems, the first triumphantly recalling God's saving actions towards Israel and the second looking forward prophetically to the nation's life in the promised land. Most of the remainder consists of homilies of one kind or another, setting out the immense importance of the law and of the need for respecting it, or warning of the dire consequences of neglecting to do so. In many ways it is this strong homiletical and admonitory material that is most typical of Deuteronomy. Laws, we may suppose, have to be formulated in accordance with the particular situations that they are designed to regulate; and we ought therefore to be wary of making too many deductions about the literary interests of the Deuteronomists from what we find in the law code. The homilies and admonitions of the framework, however, are quite unlike anything found elsewhere in the Old Testament literature. If we use this material to form a picture of the kind of persons who composed Deuteronomy, we shall be inclined to the conclusion that they were not so much law-makers as law-preachers. Cf. G. von Rad, *Studies in Deuteronomy*, p. 16; 'It is preached law'. It is the concern to elevate the status and significance of the law that is the dominant characteristic of the work.

Before examining specific passages of the Introduction and Epilogue it may be helpful to note two of the issues which have particularly attracted the attention of scholars. The first concerns the purely formal observation that the material of the framework regularly addresses itself to the reader as 'you', but sometimes in the singular and sometimes in the plural (AV indicates this, but RSV does not). Several scholars have sought to use this variation as an indication of different layers of material added to the book. More recently, however, it has been argued that, on the contrary, this variation has been introduced for purely stylistic reasons (cf. A.D. Mayes, *Comm.*, pp. 35-37). This is not to set aside the contention, which has characterised so much of the investigation into the Introduction and Epilogue of Deuteronomy, that there is evidence here of a progressive series of additions and expansions made to the original book. Such a process of growth may certainly be assumed to have occurred. But it is preferable to seek to understand this growth by examining the contents of the various parts of the book rather than by relying too much on purely formal criteria of style and language.

A second issue is that of the very elevated rhetorical style which characterizes the homilies, especially throughout chs. 4–11. As it now appears in the book, this hortatory style is a literary feature, that is, a feature connected with written composition, even though it appears to have originated in a situation where oral teaching and exhortation would have been normal. Its originators must have been preachers and teachers, rather than scribes in the narrower sense. Since it is this elevated rhetorical style that is the most disntinctive characteristic of the book of Deuteronomy, and since it also re-appears to some degree in motive clauses in the law code, it may be regarded as a major clue to the identity of its authors. This, at any rate, was a central basis of argument for G. von Rad in his form-critical analysis of the Deuteronomic material (*Studies in Deuteronomy*, pp. 11-24).

Yet another feature concerning the Introduction may be noted. The narrative of 1.1–3.29 is essentially a historical survey, couched in the form of a memoir presented by Moses to all Israel, and recounting the nation's journeyings. M. Noth (*The Deuteronomistic History*, ET JSOT Supp. 15; Sheffield: JSOT, 1981, pp. 12-17) argued that this historical survey was intended not simply as a prefatory beginning to the book of Deuteronomy, but as an opening summary of events, beginning with the revelation of God at Horeb; composed for the much longer work of Deuteronomy—2 Kings (The Deuteronomistic History). As such it formed a narrative beginning for a work that was primarily historical in character. Apart from this the book of Deuteronomy contains very little historical narrative in the full sense, but is rather a book of law, supported by a series of homilies and warnings. This suggests to the discerning reader that the introduction of this more consistently historical perspective marked a relatively late stage in the formation of the Deuteronomic literature. We can then see how the law book, which must originally have been set out in a more or less timeless fashion as the law of God for all generations of Israelites, has been given a strengthened authority, and has been modified in its character, by being given an author (Moses) and a unique and very specific historical setting. A key factor in this change of perspective was the importance attached to the mediating and revelatory work of Moses which is stressed in the Introduction.

2. **The Figure of Moses**

If we follow our general conclusion that the book of Deuteronomy has been built up by a process of supplementation and addition over a period of time, we can recognize that within this process the heightening of the importance of Moses plays a significant role. In the original law code of chs. 12–26 Moses only appears by implication in the law relating to the work of prophets in 18.15-22. In the Introduction and Epilogue, however, it is not simply that the whole is presented as having been mediated through Moses, but that this mediation is very strongly emphasized. The name of Moses appears here frequently, and with an obvious concern to stress his great importance (cf. G. von Rad, *Moses*, World Christian Books 32; London: Lutterworth, 1960, pp. 31-34).

Alongside this emphasis upon the personal mediation of Moses in procuring the revelation of the law of God, there is an accompanying interest in his work as prayerful intercessor. This is brought out in a highly reflective passage (Deut. 9.6-29), where it is stressed that, even in the period spent in the wilderness, Israel had twice come close to complete annihilation by incurring the anger of God. It is striking that in Deuteronomy this rebelliousness is viewed as primarily political in its nature and focuses upon a questioning of the human leadership that God had given to his people—cf. G.W. Coats, *Rebellion in the Wilderness* (Nashville: Abingdon, 1968, pp. 196-99). Twice Moses had interceded for the rebellious nation, even setting his own life at risk before God. The first occasion was at the time when Israel had sinned over the incident of the making of the Golden Calf (Deut. 9.16). The second time was when Israel had offended God through its unwillingness to trust him to give them victory in entering the land (9.23). On each occasion Moses had prayed and fasted throughout a period of forty days and nights so that the nation might be spared. By the recalling of these events, and their presentation in the form of an admonition from Moses, not only is the sinfulness inherent in Israel's rebelliousness brought out, but the uniqueness of the work of this great leader is brought to the fore. A quite extraordinarily high valuation is placed upon him as national leader, prayerful intercessor and man of God. He stands high above kings, priests and prophets (cf. 34.10-12).

It might at first appear that this contrast between the lack of attention to the figure of Moses in the law code and the great emphasis upon his work in the Introduction and Epilogue is no more than a reflection of the different kinds of material preserved in the separate parts of the book. However, the *degree* of this emphais suggests that something more is required to account for the change. It would seem that the emergence of a growing desire to emphasize the importance of Moses carried with it a desire to emphasize the historical setting in which Moses had served as Israel's unique mediator.

When we ask why Moses came to be seen as so important a figure in Israel's history, it becomes clear that this must be related to a further outworking of the conviction that the law of God was itself supremely important for Israel's survival. The importance of Moses came to be stressed because among the intended readers of the book there were clearly many who would have been inclined to question both the traditional authority ascribed to him and the consequent authority attaching to the law he had given. The reason why this authority should have been challenged can only be understood by considering what rival authority could have been set against it.

There was only one institution in Israel where such a rival authority could have been found. This was that of the kingship; and for the period to which we must look for the origin of Deuteronomy, this would have meant the dynastic kingship of the Davidic line. Although Deuteronomy contains only one relatively short law concerning the kingship (17.14–20), it is noteworthy that a strongly critical attitude towards this major institution is implicit in much of the book. This implied criticism does not amount to a rejection of the institution *in toto*, but rather to a concern to set it within very tight limits. That this attitude of sharp criticism towards the monarchy is implicit in Deuteronomy has been argued extensively by O. Bächli, *Israel und die Völker. Eine Studie zum Deuteronomium* (ATANT 41; Zürich: Zwingli, 1962); cf. also J.R. Porter, *Moses and Monarchy. A Study in the Biblical Tradition of Moses* (Oxford: Blackwell, 1963).

We can see from such a consideration that the great attention that is accorded to Moses in the framework to the law code of Deuteronomy is an important feature of the way in which the book presents the law as possessing a unique authority. It is a law that has been given once and for all to Israel through the leader who stands over and above all other leaders—kings, priests or prophets—who will arise within the nation. The law is therefore not open to change and modification (cf. Deut. 4.2) in the manner in which other laws of the state can be changed. In this perspective we can see how important it is to view the law code and the framework in relation to each other. The law is presented in the central code, but its authority and significance for Israel's life is explained in the speeches of the Introduction. We cannot, therefore, be content with the sharp distinction between the law code and the framework that at one time prevailed among scholars.

3. The Ten Commandments

In Deut. 5.1-2 the Introduction presents a brief report of the covenant, for which Moses had acted as mediator, made on Mount Horeb between Yahweh and Israel. This is them referred to again in Deut. 29.1 as a prior covenant-making preceeding that made in the Plains of Moab when the laws of Deuteronomy were revealed. Deut. 5.6-21 proceeds to set out the conditions of the original Horeb covenant which are repeated from Exod. 20.2-17 as the Ten

Commandments. These would, then, appear to be laws of special importance akin in many ways to basic principles of conduct, and to stand apart from, and in some degree above, the more mixed collection of laws and rulings contained in the law code. Since these Ten Commandments are also set out in Exod. 20.2-17, the fact that they are repeated in this fashion lends them a quite unique importance in the literature of the Old Testament. Before considering their special character and significance two points of literary importance need to be noted.

The first of these points concerns the priority to be accorded to one or other of the two settings (Exod. 20 and Deut. 5) where these commandments are now placed. S.R. Driver (*Comm.*, pp. 84-86) took the view, as many other scholars have done, that the Deuteronomic author has simply taken over the list of Ten Commandments from the older JE narrative of Exodus 20. Since there are some verbal differences between the two versions, notably in the sabbath commandment, this conclusion involves the supposition that some additions were subsequently made to the Exodus 20 version which were not taken over into Deuteronomy.

The second point is that most of Deut. 4.1-40 and 5.1-11.32 is built up around a concern to lend added emphasis to the first two commandments. This is a point that has been fully and helpfully elaborated by N. Lohfink, *Das Hauptgebot*. There is every reason, therefore, to recognize that the incorporation of the Ten Commandments into Deut. 5-11 has played a very important role in the formation of this entire part of the Introduction. In fact the Introduction is largely made up of a series of homilies on the first two commandments.

Certainly the very structure of the Ten Commandments, with their concise listing of ten supremely important obligations towards God and one's fellow-citizens shows a desire to highlight certain specific issues of conduct. The first four commandments list duties to God, whereas the following six concern conduct within the community.

A. Alt, in the essay referred to above, argued that the Ten Commandments represent a distinctive kind of 'apodictic' law. A special feature of Alt's observations was that the formulation of these laws as 'commandments' in which God directly addresses each individual Israelite was fundamental to their operation. They did not list separately specified penalties for infringement, because it was implied that God himself would act against the wrongdoer (as in the

case of curses; cf. Deut. 27.15-26). The compilation of a list of ten
such commandments was a teaching device, aimed at making them
readily memorable.

A. Phillips (*Ancient Israel's Criminal Law*, Oxford: Blackwell,
1970) proposed a further development and modification of this thesis
of Alt's in arguing that the Ten Commandments represent ancient
Israel's criminal law. The authority of God himself lay behind the
demand implied in each commandment, and so there was no need for
the precise penalty for breaking the commandment to be specified.
Phillips argued, however, that originally each of the issues covered
by the commandments had carried a capital penalty. In maintaining
such a view, Phillips found it necessary to claim that the original
formulation of this famous list was briefer and simpler than either of
the surviving versions in Exodus 20 or Deuteronomy 5.

This is a view that has been widely canvassed among scholars and
amounts to the claim that there was an original 'Shorter Decalogue'
(the German term *Urdekalog* is frequently used to describe this). It is
hard to escape such a conclusion, if the contention is accepted that
the listing of such Ten Commandments really is to be carried back to
the days of Moses himself (cf. H.H. Rowley, 'Moses and the
Decalogue', *Men of God. Studies in Old Testament History and
Prophecy*, London: Nelson, 1963, pp. 1-36). Some such view is more
or less essential, in any case, if the claim is to be upheld that the
Exodus 20 setting of the commandments is the original one. We have
already noted that the version set out there is longer than that of
Deuteronomy 5 and has clearly been added to later.

We may take it as certain that formulation of this special list of Ten
Commandments originally took place apart from Deuteronomy and
was designed to be used as an independent list, either orally or in
written form and very possibly both. We must ask, however, whether
it originated very much before the time of Deuteronomy. Perhaps
even more fundamental than this question of its date of origin is that
of the precise nature of these commandments. We have seen that
they are not properly formulated as laws at all, although they relate
closely to matters of religious and social conduct which are covered
by legislation. What is striking, however, is that they strive to cover
the maximum area of conduct, rather than to pinpoint very precisely
what would constitute an offence and what must then be done to the
offender. Furthermore, as Alt himself noted, they deal with matters
which, for the most part, were clearly proving difficult to deal with
through the normal processes of law. Sabbath-breaking has generally

been regarded by Jews as reprehensible, but has consistently been a matter difficult to legislate against. This was undoubtedly already the case in Old Testament times, and this strongly points us against the idea that these commandments formed a body of criminal legislation. Rather they appear to have been designed to supplement and reinforce the law, out of a recognition that it was often difficult, and sometimes impossible, to deal with matters of major religious and social importance solely through the processes of law. The burden of obedience had to be placed on each individual Israelite, whose willingness and sense of responsibility were appealed to.

This view is closely related to that of E. Gerstenberger (*Wesen und Herkunft des 'Apodiktischen Rechts'*, WMANT 20, Neukirchen-Vluyn: Neukirchener Verlag, 1965) that the Decalogue cannot properly be described as law at all, but rather represents a form of ethical demand, originating in the older clan ethic of the community of Israel. But it is not particularly important for us here to be able to trace back the origin of the distinctive commandment form. What is noteworthy is that this compilation of ten such basic demands upon conduct was brought together in order to strengthen and reinforce the religious and moral standards of ancient Israel. Most probably this occurred during a period of social upheaval and near-crisis. If so, it is wholly in accord with features that we have found elsewhere in the book of Deuteronomy.

There are good reasons, therefore, for concluding that the list of Ten Commandments originated not long before the book of Deuteronomy itself in its earliest form. The commandments show features of common concern with much that is evident in the law code of Deuteronomy, and, as we have seen, are very closely linked with the speeches of exhortation in Deut. 4–11.

Of course, this is not to suppose that the matters dealt with in the commandments were previously left unchecked prior to this time. Far from it! It was a matter of greatest concern to those who formulated the list to bring together matters that had been consistently and deeply felt to be important to the overall welfare of Israel. In this sense the Ten Commandments can be seen to represent a part of the truly 'Mosaic' inheritance of Israel since they concern matters that pertain to the basic religious commitment and social wellbeing of the nation.

When we reflect upon the question of the date of origin of the Ten Commandments, therefore, we are not seeking to discover when the particular issues dealt with first came to be matters of Israelite concern. Rather it is the bringing together of these issues and the making of them into a matter of primary, and ultimate, commitment to Yahweh as God that is the innovative element in such a list. Undoubtedly the separate matters of religious and moral behaviour which they cover had already been of deep concern to Israelite life from a much earlier period.

We may summarize our conclusions concerning the listing of the Ten Commandments in Deut. 5.6-21 and their relationship to the list of similar commandments that appears earlier in Exod. 20.2-17 in the following way:

1. The list in Deut. 5 is the older version of the two lists.
2. At one time such a list of ten primary commandments existed as a separate formulation for use in teaching, both in a domestic context as well as a religious (cultic) one.
3. It is possible that such a list existed at one time in a shorter form. (It is often claimed that they must all once have been set out as brief prohibitions). However, since we have no positive knowledge of this, such a speculative conclusion is of little help or value.
4. The inclusion of the list in Deut. 5 as a setting out of the conditions of the covenant made between God and Israel on Mount Horeb was intended to draw maximum attention to these commandments.
5. The issues dealt with in the Ten Commandments were matters of deep concern to the Deuteronomists as a group; and this is highlighted by the way in which the homilies of Deut. 4-11 elaborate further on the significance of the first two commandments.

As a general point we cannot fail to recognize the significance of the conclusion that the Ten Commandments, which have formed so important a legacy of the religious and social meaning of the Old Testament, are to be seen as a product of the Deuteronomic movement. This was a point noted as far back as 1927 by S. Mowinckel (*Le Décalogue*, Paris: Gabalda, 1927), but not adequately appreciated because it was assumed that the list in Exod. 20.2-17 was based on an older version.

4. The Speeches of Exhortation

Most of Deut. 5-11 consists of speeches of exhortation and admonition, setting out the primary importance of the law, the conviction that loyalty to God can only be shown by maintaining respect for this law, and warning of the never ceasing temptation to be neglectful of it. As these speeches now stand, the law that comes first to mind as their subject is that of the Ten Commandments set out in 5.6-21. However, A.D. Mayes (*Comm.*, pp. 39, 160ff.) follows N. Lohfink in concluding that it is not these commandments that formed the original basis for the understanding of 'law' in these chapters. They have been introduced at a relatively late stage into the Introduction —a stage which Mayes links with a 'Deuteronomistic' layer of editorial addition. If this is so then the earliest stratum of these speeches was concerned with the laws of Deut. 12.1-26.15 and was designed to draw attention to both the blessings and the temptations of life in the land promised to the ancestors. So the same theme is elaborated further, spelling out the many temptations that will flow from the diverse and dangerous religious traditions which Israel will experience in the land (7.1-6, 12-16, 17-26; 8.1-10, 11-20). What is at first striking is the extraordinary degree of repetitiveness, and the vigorous and lively illustrations with which these homilies illustrate the intensity of the temptations that will be encountered when living in the land that is about to be conquered. Clearly, the preachers who delivered these sermons in the name of Moses knew only too well how widely Israel's religious loyalties would be stretched, and how sorely its commitment to Yahweh would be tested, when settled on the soil of Canaan.

A special interest attaches to the short affirmation in 7.6-11 which emphasises certain basic theological tenets regarding Israel's divine election (cf. further below in Chapter 5). At the same time this passage recognizes that these powerful theological assertions call for fuller explanation, so that the author is compelled to fall back on an appeal to the ultimate mystery and unquestionable authority of God himself (7.8). The same theme recurs in 9.4 where attention is drawn to the wickedness of the other nations as further explanation for Israel's unique calling.

Consistently throughout these speeches the fundamental paradigm of the power and action of God is seen in Israel's deliverance from Egypt (5.6, 15; 6.12, 21; 7.8, 15, 18; 8.14; 11.3-4). This is the act of liberation and of divine love which demonstrates more than any other the nature of God and his will towards Israel.

It is in line with this triumphalist theology which dominates the homilies of chs. 5-11 that the theme of Israel's rebelliousness is introduced in 9.6-29. The majesty and power of God show up all the more brightly when set against the vacillating weakness and rebelliousness of the people upon whom he had lavished such love.

5. The Blessings and Curses

When we turn to consider the themes that are introduced in the Epilogue we may note that a particularly conspicuous one is that of blessing and curse. This largely dominates the material in chs. 27-30, although this material is not all of one kind. In order to appreciate the solemnity and seriousness of such blessings and curses it is important to keep in mind the immense power and significance that was believed to be attached to the spoken word in antiquity.

A word once uttered, and when backed up by the solemn invocation of a divine name, was believed to acquire a measure of self-fulfilling potency. In the form of a curse it could therefore be used to bring harm upon a person who might otherwise be unidentfied, or whose offence was hidden from public knowledge. This is well brought out in the dodecalogue (group of twelve) of curses in Deut. 27.15-26, which was designed to be publicly proclaimed by levitical priests. This covers twelve classes of anti-social and irreligious behavior, all of which reflect actions and activities which would normally be carried out in private and so would not easily be detected. This list bears all the marks of being a very ancient formulation which, like the Ten Commandments of 5.6-21, serves to bolster the effectiveness of the law code of chs. 12-26.

There then follows a series of blessings (28.1-14) followed by curses in (28.15-19) setting out the good or bad fortunes which would befall Israel, according to whether or not it was obedient to the law. This list of curses is then elaborated further still in 28.20-68. More descriptions of life under either blessing or curse then appear in 30.1-20.

There are two points of special importance relating to these seemingly rather heavily stressed lists of blessings and curses set in the Epilogue of Deuteronomy. The first of these is the evident fact that such listings of good and bad fortunes, and their respective association with obedience and disobedience to the law, established a coherent and rational system of experiential thought. The path of blessing embraced good health, prosperity, victory in battle and everyday security; conversely the path of curse comprised disease, death, defeat in battle and poverty. In this way life was presented as the outworking of an ordered, reasoned and intelligible whole in which the knowledge of the law provided the key to understanding the misfortunes and mysteries of daily experience.

In this way the Deuteronomists left little room for fear of malevolent spirits, or other unaccountable experiences of evil; nor is there any place for any wholly non-moral agencies of disaster which might react to the infringement of a taboo. All forms of blessing and curse have been set squarely under the umbrella of the known law of God, and all life's experiences are to be understood in the light of this law (cf. especially Deut. 29.29).

The second point concerns the close comparison which can be made between many of the features contained in these lists of curses and the lists of curses which are to be found in the ancient Near Eastern vassal treaties. This similarity has understandably provided a basis for the claim that these sections in the Epilogue to the Deuteronomic law book reflect a direct dependence on the form of such vassal treaties (so, among others, M.G. Kline and P.C. Craigie). There may well have been some degree of assimilation of the form of Deuteronomy to that of such treaties, although this cannot explain the whole of the contents of the blessing and curse sections that we now have.

We should not, therefore, draw the conclusion that the presence of such blessings and curses in the Epilogue of Deuteronomy is wholly due to such purely formal considerations. Blessing and curse, and especially fear of the latter, formed a far too deeply rooted and widely recognized aspect of life for this to have been the case. In antiquity, the possibilities of misfortune which might affect any person came in a wide range of largely predictable forms. In Deuteronomy what is especially important is the way in which such lists serve to lend added significance to the knowledge of Yahweh's law. This law has become a central guide for life, providing a revealed body of knowledge by which all persons were enabled to understand their experience of life, whether good or ill. In time it appears that this Deuteronomic basis of explanation for good or evil fortune proved to be too rigid and all-embracing to offer a fully satisfactory explanation of human fortunes. Nevertheless, over against a belief in the existence of wholly unpredictable powers and manifestation of good and evil, it served to make life intelligible, and to free human beings from the fear of such hostile forces and from the search for entirely a-moral ways of achieving health and blessing. When we compare it with the forbidding and shadowy figure of 'Death' in the shape of the god Mot as recognized in Canaanite religion, we can see how imperative was the Deuteronomic claim that the law offered a path to life:

> loving the Lord your God, obeying his voice, and cleaving to him; for that means life to you and length of days, that you may dwell in the land. . . (Deut. 30.20).

6. The Poems of Moses

The concluding part of the Epilogue in chs. 31–34 is dominated by two long poems, the Song of Moses in 32.1-43, which is introduced in 31.30, and the Blessing of Moses in 33.2-29. Before these can be seen as fitting concluding celebrations of God's power and actions on behalf of Israel, some important information is given in ch. 31 concerning what was to be done with the book of the law, once Moses had departed from the scene. Three provisions are made: first that Joshua should be commissioned to succeed Moses as the leader of Israel during the impending conquest of the land (31.7-8, 14-15, 23; cf. 34.9). Secondly provision is made for Moses himself to write down the law, which hitherto has been presented as spoken to the assembled people (31.9, 24). Thirdly the written copy of the law is then to be placed in the custody of the levitical priests, with the indication that it is essentially a religious law and that the whole of it should be read publicly once every seven years during the celebration of the Feast of Tabernacles (Booths; Deut. 31.10). Meanwhile it is to be kept safe beside the ark of the covenant in the sanctuary (31.26). It is surprising that provision for the public reading of the law is made at such an infrequent interval as once every seven years. However, this is envisaged as a formal public reading to be received alongside the daily commitment to ponder and reflect upon the meaning of the law in every home (so especially 6.7-9).

The poem entitled the Song of Moses is clearly an independent composition, and would appear to have been composed at a quite early date, probably somewhat earlier than the seventh century BC. It celebrates God's actions towards Israel, praising the greatness of his power and the justice and faithfulness of his ways (32.3-4). It is notable for a number of the themes which it introduces.

Prominent among these is the affirmation that when God (the 'Most High'-Heb. *El-'Elyon*) allocated to each of the nations their inheritance (i.e. their respective territories) he reserved his own special heritage for Jacob, who formed his own special people (32.7-9). This expresses a theological viewpoint which recognizes that each nation has its own deity, and that these nations are themselves numbered according to the number of the sons of God (32.8). However, the highest of all Gods, Yahweh, is the God of Israel alone. While pointing to the supremacy of Yahweh in the realm of gods, this mythological picture nonetheless allows some recognizable place to a number of other gods.

The other theme that is particularly striking in this poem is that of Israel's rebelliousness (vv. 15-18), which is claimed to have been shown by the people's sacrificing to demons (v. 17). Inevitably such rebellion called forth the stern judgment of God (vv. 19-25). The poem proceeds to explain that this judgment was inflicted through the agency of those who were 'no people' (v. 21), and was devastating in its effect. Only after an inner struggle did God relent from bringing about a full destruction of the people (vv. 26-35). Thereafter the poem affirms that God had determined to afford help and deliverance to his people.

So in this poem the Deuteronomists see their nation to be poised between divine judgment and mercy. The people have deserved the punishment of God's anger, but they nonetheless trust, through the lessons of the past, to receive his patient mercy. Even so, the future that is set before the people in this poem is an open one—judgment cannot be discounted and the punitive effects of God's wrath may yet prevail.

The poem entitled the Blessing of Moses in Deuteronomy 33 bears a very close resemblance to the Blessing of Jacob in Gen. 49.2-27. Like the Song of Moses it appears to have been an early composition. Appropriately, it prepares for the announcement of Moses' death in ch. 34. It surveys the character and achievements of each of the tribes of Israel, giving much vitally interesting information about the earliest phase of Israel's national life and the origins of the nation. It perceives the varied characteristics of each of the tribes and relates their respective fortunes to these. It is both a prophecy and a historical survey.

With these poems and the brief account of the death of Moses the Epilogue to the Deuteronomic law code is brought to an end; and with it the entire literary composition of the Pentateuch also comes to its close. The work of Moses is ended and his legacy has been granted to the world. By celebrating the greatness of Moses in this way, the framework material of Deuteronomy also point afresh to his dominating role in the entire Pentateuch.

Further Reading

The framework to Deuteronomy has been the subject of several major studies. Among recent works that by N. Lohfink, *Das Hauptgebot. Eine Untersuchung literarischer Einleitungsfragen zu Dtn. 5-11*, Analecta Biblica 20, Rome; Biblical Institute Press, 1963, has been particularly influential. Although it is only available in German, many of the issues that it raises are discussed extensively in the commentary by A.D. Mayes. For the Ten Commandments the following general books are helpful: J.J. Stamm and M.E. Andrew, *The Ten Commandments in Recent Research* (SBT Second Series 2), London: SCM, 1967; E. Nielsen, *The Ten Commandments in New Perspective* (SBT Second Series 7), London: SCM, 1968. Cf. also W. Harrelson, *The Ten Commandments and Human Rights*, Philadelphia: Fortress, 1980.

On the curses the following may be helpful: S. Gevirtz, 'West Semitic Curses and the Problem of the Origins of Hebrew Law', *VT* 11, 1961, pp. 137-58; D.R. Hillers, *Treaty Curses and the Old Testament Prophets*, Biblical et Orientalia 16, Rome: Biblical Institute Press, 1964; On the Mosaic poems see C.J. Labuschagne, 'The Song of Moses: Its Framework and Structure', *De Fructu Oris Sui. Essays in Honour of A. van Selms*, ed. I.H. Eybers, F.C. Fensham, C.J. Labuschagne, W.C. van Wyk, A.H. van Zyl, Leiden: Brill, 1971, 85-98; G.E. Wright, 'The Lawsuit of God: A Form-critical Study of Deuteronomy 32', *Israel's Prophetic Heritage*, ed. B.W. Anderson and W. Harrelson, London: SCM, 1962, pp. 26-67.

An older work that covers the material in the light of an earlier stage of criticism is A.C. Welch, *Deuteronomy: The Framework to the Code*, Oxford: Oxford University Press, 1932.

5

THE CENTRAL
THEOLOGICAL THEMES

O NE OF THE MOST striking of all the features of the book of
Deuteronomy is the way in which all of the material which it
contains in both the law code and the framework shows evidence of
having been composed in conformity to certain basic theological ideas.
More distinctive even than the style of the Deuteronomists is the fact
that what they have written appears to have been expressed within a
carefully thought-through theological framework. Much that is to be
found particularly in the homilies in chs. 5–11 has been intentionally
framed in order to stress these theological ideas. The Deuteronomists
were undoubtedly the most theologically self-conscious and ideo-
logically aware of any of the major schools of writers who have
contributed to the Old Testament. For this reason S. Herrmann ('Die
konstruktive Restauration. Das Deuteronomium als Mitte biblischer
Theologie', *Probleme biblischer Theologie, von Rad Festschrift*, ed.
H.W. Wolff; Munich: Beck, 1971, pp. 155-70) has argued that it is the
Deuteronomic theology that marks the ideological centre of the Old
Testament. Certainly there is no other comparable body of Old
Testament literature which displays anything like the same coherence
and assertiveness with regard to its theological ideas. Combined with
this is the fact that this Deuteronomic theology has obviously been
directed at countering a number of prevalent ideas in the popular
thought and practice of ancient Israel. Further, there is also
observable a clear educational intention: to teach certain truths
about God and the nature of Israel's worship of him, which were
being seriously neglected. It is important therefore in any study of
the book of Deuteronomy that the attention given to these basic
theological ideas should be carefully highlighted. Foremost among
them was a concern with the nature and identity of God himself.

1. **God**

It is appropriate that the study of the central theological themes of Deuteronomy should begin with its doctrine of God. All that the book teaches about the nature of true religion, the dangers of alien traditions of worship, and the possibility of human communion with God derives from this central doctrine. Moreover the Deuteronomic authors show every sign of having arrived at their doctrine of God after prolonged and careful reflection. More than anywhere else in the Old Testament Deuteronomy shows an awareness of the truth that all worthy forms of religion must be founded upon a theology—a word, or doctrine, concerning the nature of God.

It is this consciousness of the need for a right understanding of God that permeates the powerful opening affirmation of the Shema: 'Hear, O Israel, The Lord our God is one Lord...' (Deut. 6.5). This affirmation concerning the oneness of God is not quite monotheism in the full sense, although it comes close to it and has frequently been understood by Jewish and Christian interpretators as implying such a doctrine. What it asserts is that Yahweh, the Lord God of Israel, is one single God. He does not exist in many different forms in different sanctuaries; neither is he simply the head of a pantheon of gods who in other respects share his nature, without enjoying equivalent status. The notion of a hierarchy of deities, with the chief of them celebrated as 'King of the gods' was a widespread feature of the religious traditions of the ancient Near East. Certainly this was the case in the varied types of Canaanite religion which had characterized the worship of the pre-Israelite occupants of the land. All the indications are that these traditions of worship and ritual had continued to hold a powerful fascination for the people of Israel right up to the late seventh century BC when Deuteronomy was composed.

To what extent this categorical affirmation by the Deuteronomists of the oneness of Yahweh the God of Israel approximates to a concept of monotheism requires very careful attention. It affirms that there is only one Yahweh, but it does not make any categorical denial that other deities with other names exist. Elsewhere their existence is clearly assumed in the book (cf. especially Deut. 32.9). However, the entire context of the affirmation in Deut. 6.5 makes it clear that Yahweh is superior to all other gods in his power and his love. It is made absolutely plain that there is no other god like him, even if it is not stated that there is no other God. In many respects it is this bold claim that marks the most important feature of monotheism so far as the Bible is concerned; hence it has often been described as a form of practical monotheism.

What is affirmed by such a doctrine is that Yahweh is superior to all other gods and that, in his essential nature, he is imcomparable among all that human beings worship in the divine realm (cf. especially the excellent treatment in C.J. Labuschagne, *The Incomparability of Yahweh in the Old Testament*, Leiden: Brill, 1966, pp. 114ff.). It is the sense of a threat to this essential truth concerning the oneness and uniqueness of Yahweh as God that motivates the harsh treatment which Deuteronomy prescribes for those who previously occupied the land and worshipped other deities:' You must utterly destroy them. . . For they would turn away your sons from following me to serve other gods' (Deut. 7.1-5).

Surprisingly, rather less is said by the Deuteronomists than might have been expected concerning what it was about these other gods, especially the cults of Baal and Ashtaroth, which was so objectionable. The most forthright polemic is directed against their use of images to represent gods and goddesses, and this is, in itself, understood to be a misrepresentation of the true nature of deity. In general the widespread use of visual symbols, and in particular the use of standing pillars of stone and of erect wooden poles, conveyed strongly sexual associations. However for the Deuteronomists it is the very idea that any physical object, whatever its form and whatever symbolism it conveyed, could represent the presence and power of God that is rejected (cf. especially Deut. 5.8). It is taken for granted that any image of deity points to a false god and misrepresents the truth concerning the divine nature and sovereign power.

In the long speech of Deut. 4.1-40 the apologetic unit in vv. 9-24 presents the fullest defence in the Old Testament of this vigorous hostility to the use of images in worship (only Isa. 44.9-20 is comparable to it). The Deuteronomic objection is that, when God revealed his will to Israel at Mount Horeb in the form of the law and in the making of the covenant, he was hidden in fire, and no form was visible (Deut. 4.12, 15-19). However, such an affirmation touches only the surface of the Deuteronomic doctrine of God, since the more fundamental antagonism towards the use of images clearly lies, not in the historical form of the revelation that Israel has received, but in the sense that such images impugn the sovereignty of God. A deity whose image can be held and manipulated by human beings cannot truly be God.

There is furthermore in Deuteronomy a deep and pervasive awareness that it is not physical objects, or even holy places and ritual actions, which in themselves make possible human communion with God. Such communion is conceived as altogether too inward, spiritual and personal for this to be the case. It can only come about through God's reaching out to his creatures and through their response in turning to him in love and gratitude. Communion with God must embrace thought, feeling and will if it is to be an effective contact between the divine and human realms. Without this personal turning, seeking and loving God there can be no genuine relationship with him. It is for this reason that the affirmation concerning the oneness of God is followed up with the words: 'and you shall love. . . . ' (Deut. 6.5). The true altar where a transaction with God can take place is the human heart, so that the physical sanctuary with its rituals can be no more than an aid towards facilitating this more inward contact with God.

The primary consequence of this passionately held doctrine of God in Deuteronomy is its vigorously upheld restriction of sacrificial worship to one single sanctuary which it describes as 'the place which Yahweh your God will choose out of all your tribes to put his name and make his habitation there' (Deut. 12.5. This law of the sanctuary in Deut. 12.1-14 is a much developed and modified expansion of the older law of the altar in Exod. 20.24). Much discussion has taken place on the question whether this Deuteronomic law of the sanctuary was intended from the outset to apply to Jerusalem alone, as was clearly the case in the seventh century BC, or whether some earlier (North Israelite) sanctuary may initially have been envisaged. The subject will be dealt with below in Chapter 6 in connection with other indications of a possible North Israelite origin for features of Deuteronomy.

A further feature of this Deuteronomic doctrine of God is, in its way, even more striking and far-reaching in its theological implications. This is the fact that the sanctuary where alone sacrifices are to be offered is defined as 'the place which Yahweh your God will choose to *put his name* and make his habitation there' (Deut. 12.5). The concept of the name of God, serving as the representation of God's presence in the sanctuary, has undoubtedly been developed out of the older idea that the altar was the place where God's name was invoked (cf. Exod. 20.24). But the Deuteronomic authors have sought to avoid too crude a notion of the idea that God's presence (Heb. *panim* = face, person) could, in some mysterious way, be located at the sanctuary. They have sought to emphasise the fact that God's true place of habitation could only be in heaven; his being invoked in the sanctuary was made possible, however, by his setting his name there as a form of representation of his Being. In this fashion the invoking of the name at the sanctuary completely obviates any excuse for the use of an image to make access to God possible. The entire development marks a very bold step towards the spiritualizing and personalizing of the understanding of worship (cf. especially G. von Rad, *Studies in Deuteronomy*, pp. 37-44; T.N.D. Mettinger, *The Dethronement of Sabaoth. Studies in the Shem and Kabob Theologies*, CB Old Testament Series 18; Lund: Gleerup, 1982). Overall therefore the Deuteronomic doctrine of God puts a great deal of weight upon ideas of his personal nature, his transcendence above all other gods and creatures, and his uniqueness and distinctness from all those other beings that people call gods and goddesses.

We must certainly accept that, in the various traditions of Canaanite religion, the notion that the same deity could be present at several sanctuaries, all of which were dedicated to his worship, had encouraged the belief that there were in reality many Baals and many forms of the goddess Astarte, even though, as we know from the Canaanite mythology reflected in the texts from ancient Ugarit, there was essentially only one Baal. However, the modern interpreter finds the particular roles and relationships of the gods and goddesses of ancient Ugarit, which reveal much of the character of Canaanite religion, very difficult to construe.

We must regard this Deuteronomic development of the doctrine of God as the fullest and most significant of all the theological turning-points in the concept of deity which the Old Testament brings to our attention. At one stroke it combines ideas of divine transcendence, incorporeality, invisibility and universal sovereignty, and so breaks dramatically with the religious traditions which preceeded it, and which appear to have prevailed for so long in the ancient Near Eastern world. God is made to appear altogether more distinct, more other-worldly and more personal in his nature than in the older literature of the Old Testament. Such a change can only have come about as the result of a prolonged period of reflection and re-examination of traditional ideas in the circle which produced the Deuteronomic writings.

It is in accordance with this Deuteronomic theology of the divine name that the ark, which had earlier been the most prominent of the physical expressions of God's presence and power in Israel, should now also undergo a measure of re-interpretation. The ark is now described solely in terms of being a container, in the form of a box, in which the tablets of the law were kept (Deut. 10.1-5; 31.26). This contrasts markedly with the older pre-Deuteronomic sense of God's very presence being indissolubly linked with the ark (cf. Num. 10.35ff.; 1 Sam. 4.5-11). Further consequences of this important development in the doctrine of God by the Deuteronomists are to be seen in the heavy emphasis that is placed upon God's dwelling in heaven in the prayer for the dedication of the temple of Solomon in 1 Kgs 8.22-53. This prayer is certainly to be regarded as having been composed by an author who was fully and deeply in agreement with the doctrine of God propounded by Deuteronomy. He has used the occasion of the prayer as an opportunity for explaining how the idea of a temple could be accepted alongside such an exalted doctrine of God as the Deuteronomists had expressed. To this extent they sought to establish a theology of the holy place which broke with the older symbolism and terminology which thought of temples as 'houses' where the deity dwelt.

We have already touched upon the fact that it is the Deuteronomic doctrine of God which has given rise to the harshest feature of the teaching of the book. This is the fervent and repeated insistence upon the total destruction of all the altars, cult-symbols and sanctuaries of the gods formerly worshipped in the land (Deut. 12.2-3). Even a prophet, or a close relative, a son, a daughter or a wife, who dared to suggest to another Israelite that he, or she, should turn to the worship of some other god was to be dealt with without mercy (Deut. 13.1-5, 6-10). Death by stoning is the prescribed punishment for such a religious offence (Deut. 12.10f.). Even whole cities were to be given over to destruction if all its inhabitants had been enticed away to the worship of another god (12.12-18). Although it is something of a relief to realise that this barbarous condemnation of alien worshippers and deities was, in historical reality, largely hypothetical and theoretical, its severity in intention cannot be ignored. No modern interpreter, sensitive to the centuries of religious intolerance that have brought so much needless suffering to the world, can any longer support such an attitude. Nevertheless, its incorporation into so central a place in the teaching of Deuteronomy shows how sharply contested was the need to establish a clear and consistent doctrine of God. It also brings to light the sense of crisis that pervades much of this book. The Deuteronomic authors firmly believed that the national disasters which had overtaken their nation were the consequence of the fact that God's anger had been aroused against the entire nation on account of its indifference to its inherited religious loyalty. They now felt passionately that the time had come for all the remaining vestiges of these ancient rites and traditions to be removed.

There has been much serious discussion whether this Deuteronomic teaching did in fact represent an almost complete innovation imposed upon a people who had grown up in an atmosphere of very mixed religious loyalties and traditions. It has been strongly argued that the Deuteronomists were in fact doing no more than to intensify a feature of Israelite faith that had its origins in the work of Moses himself centuries before the time when Deuteronomy was written. Both positions can claim some measure of support from the evidence of archaeology.

Overall we can see that Deuteronomy puts forward a very coherent and vehemently expressed doctrine of God. It did so in an age when its authors were conscious that the very survival of Israel as a nation was under the most serious threat. Its doctrine of God is thus inseparably linked to its doctrine of the nature and identity of Israel as a people.

2. The Doctrine of Israel

If the doctrine of God marks the foundation of the faith of the Deuteronomists, then certainly it is the doctrine of Israel that stands as the fullest complement to it. We have noted that the words of the Shema commence with the invocation: 'Hear, O Israel: Yahweh our God is one Yahweh' (Deut. 6.5). Such a call presupposes that Israel exists as a clearly defined entity to be addressed, and that God himself can be described by this people as 'our' God. Deuteronomy in fact makes certain very clear assumptions about Israel which pervade the entire book. Israel can be defined as a nation (Heb. *goy*; cf. *TDOT*, II, pp. 426-33). It has a positively recognized central government in the kingship (Deut. 17.14-20), and it dwells in a land which, it claimed, had been promised to its ancestors (cf. especially Deut. 6.1; 7.1). This concept of the land as a divine gift to the nation, which constitutes its 'heritage' very much in the manner that a family, or clan, looked upon its smallholding as such an inherited gift, forms a very prominent and distinctive feature of all that Deuteronomy understands by 'Israel'. It is the most precious of all the benefits that Israel's knowledge of God has brought to it. The sense of crisis that we have mentioned as present in much of the book, especially in the homilies of chs. 5–11, is very directly related to this concern with the land. (The entire subject of the land in Deuteronomy is dealt with very fully in the study of P. Diepold, *Israel Land*, BWANT 95; Stuttgart: Kohlhammer, 1972). Without a land, Israel's national existence would effectively be brought to an end.

A further feature of what Deuteronomy has to say about the nature of Israel is carefully incorporated into the very form and style of the book. As we have noted, this is presented as a speech addressed to 'all Israel', who are pictured, rather unrealistically, as gathered together in their entirety before setting out on the conquest of the land. The title 'all Israel' is one which is strongly emphasised in Deuteronomy and has clearly been chosen out of a knowledge that this unity had been sorely tried and tested through the nation's experiences. In fact we are forced to the conclusion that such a title was used precisely because the authors were well aware that, since the time of Solomon's death, the nation had been broken apart into two separate kingdoms. Undoubtedly this disruption of the unity of the people of Israel, which brought about the existence of the two sister kingdoms of Israel and Judah, is viewed as constituting a serious act of disobedience. In the eyes of the Deuteronomists Israel is a single people whose unity derives from God himself, since it is his will that has made them a people. Hence disunity is disobedience, and Deuteronomy is quite unequivocal about this.

In spite of the clear recognition that Israel is a nation, living on the land given to it by God, the image that is presented of the nation is more that of a family, or clan, than of a nation with all its mixed and varied elements. In consequence all Israelites are encouraged to think of themselves as 'brothers' (cf. Deut. 14.7; 15.2, 3).

There are two major theological ideas by which the Deuteronomists present their understanding of the manner in which Israel, as a nation, is related to God. These are the concepts of election and covenant. Both of these concepts would appear to be developments and adaptations of ideas that had been in use earlier in rather different contexts. What the Deuteronomists have done is to broaden the range of their application and to define more precisely what such concepts imply. A further feature is also relevant to both concepts. This is that, in spite of the considerable clarity and emphasis with which these ideas are set out, it seems clear that it was in the process of building up and elaborating the Deuteronomic doctrine of Israel that each of these themes was introduced. We shall deal first with that of Yahweh's *election of Israel*, since this concept is expressed primarily at one single point in the book: Deut. 7.6-11 (cf. also Deut. 14.2). Deut. 7.6-8a reads:

> For you are a people holy to Yahweh your God; Yahweh your God has chosen you to be a people for his own possession, out of all the peoples that are on the face of the earth. It was not because you were more in number than any other people that Yahweh set his love upon you and chose you, for you were the fewest of all peoples; but it is because Yahweh loves you.

What is strikingly evident here is that the concept of Israel's having been uniquely chosen by God is firmly related to the entire nation, and is not mediated through the kingship or the land. Israel as an entire people has been the object of the divine choice. Further, there is a firm recognition that such a concept of divine election calls for some explanation to show why Israel is the chosen people in preference to other nations. In the end we may recognize that simply to place the emphasis upon the mysterious action of the divine love does not, of itself, properly resolve the difficulty, but merely sets it in a different frame of reference. Nevertheless there is a clear acceptance that Yahweh's choice of Israel must be related in some fashion to the fact that he is also responsible for the being and destiny of other nations. The subject is dealt with more fully in Th. C. Vriezen, *Die Erwählung Israels nach dem AT*, ATANT 24; Zürich: Zwingli, 1953; cf. also H. Seebass in *TDOT*, II, 73-87.

The doctrine of covenant in Deuteronomy first appears in ch. 5, where the Ten Commandments follow as the specific conditions or 'terms' of this covenant.

> Yahweh our God made a covenant with us in Horeb. Not with our fathers did Yahweh make this covenant, but with us, who are all of us here alive this day (Deut. 5.2).

The idea of covenant is then further elaborated in ch. 29 where the covenant in the plains of Moab is set out as another, parallel covenant to that made at Horeb. Already we have noted in our examination of the form and structure of Deuteronomy that several important studies have made very close comparisons between the form of the book and that of ancient Near Eastern vassal-treaties. Taken with due caution, and recognizing that such an adaptation of the form of Deuteronomy to that of such treaties appears only to have been a relatively late development in the growth and editing of the book, we may agree that such an assimilation has taken place.

This would accord with the contention of L. Perlitt, *Bundestheologie im Alten Testament*, WMANT 36, Neukirchen-Vluyn: Neukirchener Verlag, 1969, that such a covenant theology represents a Deuteronomistic, rather than a properly Deuteronomic, development (for the significance of this, see below under Chapter 7 (§2). The theme of covenant in the Old Testament has been the subject of very extensive discussion; its relevance for the Deuteronomic understanding of Israel may be set out briefly. Clearly a primary purpose of such a doctrine was to add further emphasis to the belief that God's relationship to his people Israel was a contingent one. It was not a 'natural', or indissoluble, bond but one that was conditioned through the law that God had given. Furthermore, by stressing this contingent covenant nature of the bond between God and nation, the Deuteronomic movement gave a major place to the law which is the centrepiece of the Deuteronomic literature. The law represents the 'conditions' of the covenant, which Israel is placed under an obligation to observe, in the same way that a suzerain power imposed specific treaty obligations upon a vassal. The concept of covenant thereby gave importance and status to the concept of law, a feature which is very marked in Deuteronomy. In many ways it is the fact that the Deuteronomic understanding of law cannot be comprehended within the confines of other ancient Near Eastern law codes that makes the recognition of the covenant form of Deuteronomy a significant one.

As with the idea of election, there has been much discussion whether or not the Deuteronomic doctrine of covenant rests upon earlier precedents in Israelite thought. It is the contention of E.W. Nicholson, *God and His People*, Oxford: Oxford University Press, 1985, that it does. There can be no question, however, that, in developing the idea of covenant in the way they did, the Deuteronomists accorded to it a much increased theological significance as a definition of the meaning of Israel's unique claim to a relationship to Yahweh as its God. By combining the ideas of a national divine election with those of an ongoing covenant bond between them, the Deuteronomists found a means of maintaining the claim that Yahweh's power extends over all peoples, whilst also retaining the earlier belief that he is nevertheless uniquely the god of Israel. Faith has risen beyond national boundaries, without yet reaching to a full and complete monotheistic universalism.

Before leaving the study of the highly important Deuteronomic doctrine of Israel as the people of God, we must look at the very significant law of the king in Deut. 17.14-20. This is unique in the Bible as the only attempt to present a constitutional definition of the king's role and status. It also clearly marks out the Deuteronomic literature as stemming from a time when Israel still possessed a king, or at least was fully expecting to do so. In this short statement about the position of such a monarchy we may draw attention to the following features. In the first place it is strongly stressed that the king is to be 'one from among your brethren' (Deut. 17.15), thereby ruling out the possibility of a foreigner holding such an office, but also at the same time sweeping aside any belief that the king was a semi-divine, or uniquely endowed, being. He is merely human, although his approval by God and his right to the kingship are expressed through the formula of divine selection (v. 15). How this selection will manifest itself is not made fully explicit; but it should certainly not be discounted that the authors intended by such a doctrine to point to some idea of dynastic principle. This is certainly how the kingship of Judah operated in regard to the family of David, and it is made abundantly clear in the Deuteronomistic editing of the books of 1 & 2 Samuel and 1 & 2 Kings that such a divine choice had been revealed in the case of David and his heirs (so especially 2 Sam. 7.1-17).

This presentation of the role of the king in Deuteronomy represents an important endorsement of an institution which elsewhere receives considerable criticism in the Old Testament literature especially by the prophets (the subject is treated extensively in F. Crüsemann, *Der Widerstand gegen das Königtum. Die antiköniglichen Texte des Alten Testamentes und der Kampf um den frühen israelitischen Staat*, WMANT 49, Neukirchen-Vluyn, 1978). As a nation Israel requires a fully organized and effective government. Only so can it fulfil the requirements of living according to the law's demands. In other respects, however, much of the ideology of Israel as a nation presented by Deuteronomy reflects the values and ties of a community of tribes. This has led G.E. Wright ('Deuteronomy', *IB*, Vol. II, pp. 324-26), to view the Deuteronomic concept of Israel as stemming directly from that of the old pre-monarchic tribal federation, centred at Shechem. But this is to project back into that early period features of Deuteronomy which must clearly have originated much later and which have been profoundly affected by all that Israel had experienced since the foundation of the state in the age of David and Solomon. Not only in its ideology of kingship, but in its concept of Israel as one single covenant people, and even in the understanding of the land as a divinely given gift, the book of Deuteronomy reflects some centuries of experience enjoyed by Israel as a nation, living among other nations. In so far as it does look back upon the age of Moses and the period spent in the wilderness as the paradigms for Israel's continuing life, it does so, not because these formed a 'Golden Age', but because they stood closest to the fount of revelation.

3. The Doctrine of Worship

Apart from its doctrines concerning Yahweh, the God of Israel, and Israel as the specially chosen people of God, Deuteronomy is particularly significant and far-reaching in its teaching about the meaning of worship. It is a natural and necessary consequence of the first two themes that worship, which provides a means by which deity and nation can remain in continued communion with each other, should be understood in a truly theological manner. It is worship that brings the relationship between God and people into focus and provides for Israel the continued occasion for the rediscovery of God and for displaying that degree of gratitude and love towards him which marks the proper response which he desires. So for the Deuteronomists the essence of worship is the provision of a time for Israel to reflect and reappraise its loyalty.

It is in accordance with these convictions that the book of Deuteronomy presents what is undoubtedly the most fully reasoned and consistently explained theology of worship in the Old Testament. Not until the New Testament do we find any comparable leap in the development of the understanding of the meaning and purpose of worship.

The first of the Deuteronomic innovations concerning worship is the requirement that all sacrificial offerings should be restricted to the altar of one single sanctuary (Deut. 12.5-14). We have already remarked upon the extent to which this represents a radical shift in the rules and regulations governing Israel's cultus. Prior to this legislation a wide variety of altars, located in many sanctuaries in the land, had been tolerated. Although there has been discussion whether some other shrine than that of Jerusalem may once have been envisaged in the formulation of the Deuteronomic legislation (see above, p. 28), there can be no question that in the late seventh

century BC, when the book of Deuteronomy became an effective
instrument of reform, Jerusalem was the sanctuary to which this rule
applied. This central shrine was to be the place to which all offerings
were brought (Deut. 12.6, 14) and where they were to be eaten (12.7).
The purpose of such acts is explained as that of providing an
occasion of rejoicing before God for one's family (12.12, 18), and of
giving an opportunity for the levite also to enjoy the benefits of God's
land (12.19).

The reason why ritual acts of this nature are restricted by the
Deuteronomic legislation to one single shrine is not hard to find. It is
to ensure that all such worship should be confined to the procedures
and aims which the Deuteronomists lay down as alone pleasing to
God. The existence of many sanctuaries and altars would have
enabled a variety of practices and rituals to continue which the
authors of this book clearly regarded as reprehensible. One single
sanctuary was in accord with the understanding of one single God,
and made it possible to hope for firm and careful oversight of all that
took place there. The single sanctuary is the outward expression of
purity of worship.

The practices of eating sacrifices, of rendering burnt-offerings to
God, and of presenting tithes and firstfruits to him, were certainly
practices which long antedated the rise of Israel. Israel had simply
inherited in the land of Canaan a whole plethora of such practices.
Nor is there any likelihood that there existed any clear understanding
of what such offerings achieved and how they were pleasing to God,
although many varied assumptions were evidently current. They
were seen as a kind of 'tax' demanded by God for the use of the land,
as a means of promoting life and fertility by ensuring that part of the
produce of the soil was returned to God, and as a food that the god
himself, or herself, could consume, and so gain refreshment. With
Deuteronomy all such interpretations are wholly and comprehensively
swept aside. A completely consistent, and carefully reasoned,
doctrine of sacrificial worship is presented instead in which all
offerings are seen as an established means of expressing gratitude to
God (Deut. 14.22-27). What may at first appear as a very simple and
basic doctrine of sacrifice is, in the history of religion, a relatively late
and developed one. Deuteronomy consistently and carefully spiritualises
and internalizes the understanding of worship.

It is in very much the same vein of a radical reinterpretation of the
purpose of worship that these legislators now made a full concession

over the matter of eating game, such as the gazelle and the hart, which would have been hunted (Deut. 12.15-28). The eating of these creatures was now more or less 'secularized', with only the minimal requirement that the taboo concerning not eating the blood should be maintained (Deut. 12.23). A distinction is thereby made between the sacrificial character of the offering of tithes and firstlings and the eating of meat simply because it tastes good (Deut. 12.20, 26; 15.19-23).

We must bear in mind that central to the older pattern of worship in Israel were the three major agricultural festivals celebrated in the spring, summer and early autumn (Exod. 34.18-20). The retention of these festivals by the Deuteronomists and the elucidation of their function and purpose are the subject of a careful prescription in Deut. 16.1-17. What is strikingly new in this is the joining of the ritual of Passover, which is not mentioned in the earlier Exodus calendar, with the spring celebration of the feast of Unleavened Bread (Deut. 16.1-8). Not only is this linking together of the two spring festivals a distinctive development, but it is also noteworthy that very considerable emphasis is placed upon the Passover. Whether the linking of the two festivals had already become the norm among some Israelites, or was now, for the first time, being advocated by the Deuteronomists, can only be a matter of hypothesis. Certainly it would seem that the Deuteronomic concern to give to both celebrations an integrated and connected meaning was new. Perhaps this should be seen as the major feature of the Deuteronomic interpretation and ruling.

In some respects even more far-reaching in its theological implications for all subsequent Jewish and Christian understanding of worship is the demand that the entire celebration of the Passover should be interpreted as an act of 'remembering' the event of the exodus from Egypt, through which Israel's ancestors had first experienced true freedom. The older cultic calendar had mentioned, almost as an afterthought, that it was in the spring month of Abib when the Israelites came out of Egypt (Exod. 34.18). In the Deuteronomic elaboration of the Festival Calendar this point is again mentioned (Deut. 16.1), but is then elaborated with an explanation that the very reason for eating unleavened bread is that it should serve as a reminder of the hurried flight from the land of Egypt (Deut. 16.3). Moreover the entire celebration is explained in terms of that event: 'that all the days of your life you may remember the day when you came out of the land of Egypt'. (This subject is explored more fully in its implications for worship in B.S. Childs, *Memory and Tradition in Israel*, SBT 37, London: SCM, 1962, pp. 45ff.) No such direct explanation is offered for the other festivals, but such were soon to be supplied by Jewish tradition. In this fashion all worship became essentially an act of remembering the gracious actions of God in the past. Out of an understanding of ritual as re-enactment of a past divine work, there now emerged the more inward and spiritualized understanding that all such sense of the divine activity needed to be appropriated by the mind and heart of the worshipper. Ritual was not effective automatically: it was effective only when it became a vehicle of the worshipper's own love and responsive attitude toward God. By such legislative rulings and explanation the Deuteronomists made a radical break with a vast and complex ancient world of ritual and sacral understanding of the universe. The great struggle between forces of life and death, in which the worshipper can participate by re-enacting the victory of 'Life' over 'Death', is replaced by an altogether more moral and spiritual doctrine of worship which centres upon its value as an occasion for remembering the greatness of God's actions in the past. In this way the full effect of these past divine actions would remain meaningful and beneficial in the present. In spite of the 'remembering' side of worship, therefore, the value of worship as a real contemporary expression of human communion with God is not lost sight of.

4. Social Justice

This feature of the teaching of Deuteronomy also deserves careful attention. We have already noted the fact that the central, and almost certainly the oldest, part of the book is a code of law preserved in chs. 12–26. The teaching of the book as a whole is therefore, in both a formal and practical sense, a message concerning the role of law in society. It is addressed to ordinary lay Israelites, but it addresses them with the conviction that a just social order, the fair and firm administration of a system of law, and the general quality of life available to all, rest on the willingness of all members of Israel to seek to work for that just social order. No passage of the book manifests greater passion than the exhortation which is placed after the instruction to appoint judges and officers for legal affairs in every town:

> You shall not pervert justice; you shall not show partiality; and you
> shall not take a bribe, for a bribe blinds the eyes of the wise and

subverts the cause of the righteous. Justice, and only justice, you shall follow, that you may live and inherit the land which Yahweh your God gives you (Deut. 16.19-20).

Quite clearly the Deuteronomists believed in the importance and high priority to be accorded to the fair and incorrupt adminstration of law. This is evident from the way in which the book represents a modification and extension of an already extant system of law. This shows a significant awareness of the inevitable limitations of any system based upon the application of a fixed code of written law. Some cases would prove to be too difficult to settle in this way and would need the insight and expertise of a priest (Deut. 17.8-13). Such a falling back upon the services of the cult must undoubtedly have taken its origin in the importance for many legal, commercial and family matters of the priestly witnessing of solemn oaths (cf. Exod. 22.8, 9, 11). In legal matters this particularly applied where no adequate proof of guilt could be established. Overall we can see that Deuteronomy regarded such a resort to the cultus as a kind of 'second best' means of dealing with difficult cases. If this is so, as is widely recognized, it also shows how important it was in the eyes of the Deuteronomists to strive for a rational, coherent and relatively 'secular' system of law and legal administration. To this extent principles of fairness and reason, and of the placing of the entire community under an obligation to pursue what is just, are accorded a measure of precedence, even over the services afforded by the cult.

We may recognize the same general tendency in the reasoning that underlies the instructions for the appointment of judges and officers (Deut. 16.18). These were quite evidently intended to form an experienced body of guides and legal administrators (cf. especially on this subject H.-J. Boecker, *Law and Legal Administration in the Old Testament*, pp. 57ff.). Deuteronomy was not introducing an organized system of law into Israel for the first time, but was endeavouring to establish a more comprehensive, and more systematically organized, basis for the adminstration of legal affairs that had previously prevailed within the nation. It is noteworthy that the word of authorization is addressed to the people as a whole—'you shall appoint'—(Deut. 16.18), and not to the king, who would undoubtedly up to this time have been responsible for legal innovations in Israel. To this extent Deuteronomy manifests a very marked broadening of the realm of law, and makes a strikingly important move in the direction of rendering law independent of both the royal court and the priesthood.

When we ask how justice was upheld within an ancient community like that of ancient Israel before the introduction of comprehensive systems of law we can see that, besides the monarchy and the cultic personnel, there was also a large area of concern for social justice which would have been left in the hands of individual families and clans to deal with. On this front too, Deuteronomy was concerned to implement reform and a more secure and equitable system of legal administration. Undoubtedly the Deuteronomists believed that a properly organized system of law would do much to make Israel a more just and law-abiding society.

The attempt to impose greater restrictions on the freedom of individual families and clans to take legal matters into their own hands is well exemplified by the law of Deut. 21.18-21. This is a ruling concerning the punishment of a rebellious son, whose waywardness could no doubt seriously undermine the economic strength and integrity of a family as a whole. A firm ruling is made that the case must be laid before the elders of the city for their examination, before any violent action is taken. Only then could stern punishment be meted out, initiated by the men of the city and not by the head of the family (v. 21). Even though we may feel shocked by the rigour with which the Deuteronomic authors prescribe capital punishment for such crimes as the inciting of others to worship some god other than Yahweh (Deut. 13; 5, 8-10), the aim was undoubtedly to establish a wholly just and devout community.

In the past, some scholars have been inclined to see in the book of Deuteronomy a step in the direction of establishing a religious legalism, such as emerged in later Judaism. The emphasis upon knowledge of a code of law, upon a tight legal administration and upon the embodiment of this law in a fixed written form may all be thought to have encouraged such a tendency. It would, however, be too harsh a judgement to accuse Deuteronomy of introducing a legalistic understanding of religion into ancient Israel. Its concern was rather to promote the idea and administrative effectiveness of a reasoned and fair system of law than to increase the extent to which law impinged upon everyday life. What in one set of social circumstances could be viewed as a blessing could, when circumstances were different, be exaggerated to the extent of becoming a danger.

There is an eminent note of practicality in the Deuteronomic attempt to apply the law in accordance with its inner spirit, rather than in any formal and mechanical fashion. Such is already evident in the appeals to the reader to remember that he came from a family of slaves (cf. Deut. 15.15); and the same spirit is evident in the instruction that, when a slave who had fulfilled his period of slave-service was set free, he should be given a generous share of produce and sheep in order to be able to restart as an independent citizen-farmer (Deut. 15.13-14).

It may be felt that the emphasis upon social justice and the implementation of a fair and comprehensive system of law enforcement indicates that Israel, as experienced by the Deuteronomists, had become a rather lawless community. It is not impossible that this was the case, and many scholars have felt that this aspect of the Deuteronomic teaching reflects a strong dependence upon the great prophets of the eighth century.

In reality, however, it is very difficult to make informed and firm comparisons regarding the relative social awareness of different communities at different periods. Much that Deuteronomy affirms to be of paramount importance on this front can be seen to have been issues that were widespread and persistent in the ancient world. If there was one unique factor which had led to a serious breakdown in the moral health of the society which the Deuteronomists experienced, this is likely to have been the experience of a century of Assyrian imperial control. This almost certainly brought about serious economic disruption to the community, with consequent deprivation, and appears also to have sparked off a measure of entrepreneurial greed and exploitation. It is by no means impossible that it also caused ruinous breakdowns in the vitality of family and clan life. That the very fabric of social justice was threatened, by what Israel had experienced as the 'curse' of vassaldom to Assyria for a century, could then be more adequately understood. However simplistic such an explanation may appear, it was the conviction of the Deuteronomists that this vassaldom was a mark of the punitive hand of God turning against the nation. Nor should we feel surprised that there was felt to be a close link between Israel's loss of national freedom and the consciousness of a deep social malaise that infected all aspects of its life—economic, political and religious.

Taken as a whole the teaching that Deuteronomy has to offer regarding social justice is very impressive. It was certainly based upon a confidence in the efficacy of a written code of law, administered by officials who were expected to be free from corruption and wholly loyal to the ideals of the state as propounded by the Deuteronomists. That such a body of officials would easily have been found may be thought questionable, and several critics and commentators have regarded the Deuteronomic legislation as rather idealistic and impractical. There is, nevertheless, a sense in which it was clearly very important to establish clear and firm ideas and to uphold certain basic principles, even in a very difficult and unpromising age. So often in human history some of the most valuable and influential documents of social reform and moral ideals have arisen out of periods of turmoil and social disorder.

In concluding this consideration of the Deuteronomistic concern with the idea of a just society, it may be noted that the final editorial work upon the book of Deuteronomy would appear to have taken place after the beginning of the Babylonian exile with the fall of Jerusalem to Babylonian forces in 598 BC. Probably some of it may date from after the even worse debacle of 587 BC. As a result of these political catastrophes an increasing number of those who sought to remain loyal to their calling as the people of God found themselves living in a state of exile, which rapidly passed into a state of more or less permanent dispersion. In consequence, the emphasis placed upon the ideals presented in Deuteronomy of a community that was self-monitoring in its concern with social order and wellbeing, and in which the family itself took a prime responsibility for the education of all its members (cf. Deut. 6.7-9), became of immense importance. As Judaism developed as 'the religion of a book', a process which itself owed so much to Deuteronomy, so also did it develop as a religion of a community which was no longer a nation. The deep concern with social justice which has characterised much of Jewish life emerged from within these Jewish communities as a direct expression of a concern to be loyal to God and to the conditions of the covenant which he had made with them. It was the book of Deuteronomy that drew this concern with justice into the forefront of its religious aims.

Further Reading

In addition to the literature already mentioned or referred to in the text of the chapter, the reader is referred to my small book on the theology of Deuteronomy entitled *God's Chosen People* (London: SCM, 1968). For the concept of Israel in Deuteronomy, an earlier book by G. von Rad entitled *Das Gottesvolk im Deuteronomium* (BWANT III, 11 (=36); Stuttgart: Kohlhammer, 1929) has been influential; and its consequences are to be seen in the later, and better known, writings of this author on Deuteronomy. For the theme of social justice much valuable material is to be found in L. Epsztein, *Social Justice in the Ancient Near East and the People of the Bible*, London: SCM, 1986, especially pp. 104-34.

6

AUTHORSHIP
AND HISTORICAL
BACKGROUND

W E HAVE SO FAR spoken of the authors of Deuteronomy simply
as 'the Deuteronomists', since this provides a suitably open
assessment of their identity. We have, at the same time, suggested
various features which point to the conclusion that the book emerged
in Israel some time during the seventh century BC. This has been a
widely held verdict of critical scholarship, although one that has been
subject to various provisos and modifications. It may at first appear
to be a rather uncompromising and even sceptical judgment about
the 'law book of Moses', since the whole presentation and structure
of the book clearly point us to a recognition of its claims to be an
expression of the authentic Mosaic tradition of Israel's religion. But
it would be wrong to think that there is something false or spurious
about this claim. The book's clear intention is to present to its
readers genuine information about the content of Mosaic faith and
morality; and this needs to be upheld as something quite separate
from the more narrowly critical judgment about the precise period
when this was couched in its extant literary form. The whole aura of
the book shows that it was concerned to preserve a tradition that was
old and seen by its authors as a wholly authentic testimony to what
Moses had bequeathed to Israel as his legacy. The fact that this
tradition has been given this particular literary form simply shows
that these authors sensed how the passage of time, and the
temptations that had beset Israel, had combined to obscure and
undermine what they saw as the truly Mosaic content of faith. It was
their earnest desire to present to their readers a clear and firm
picture of what the true and ancient Mosaic faith really was.

1. **The Time of Origin**

We have already noted a number of points that have a bearing on the question of the time of origin of the book of Deuteronomy. It was a major step forward in the development of modern study of the Pentateuch when, in 1805, W.M.L. de Wette suggested that the book of Deuteronomy was the law book discovered in the temple in the eighteenth year of the reign of king Josiah (639-609 BC): that is, in the year 623/622 BC. This discovery is reported very fully in 2 Kgs 22–23 in relation to some repairs carried out on the temple. As a result of the discovery a very far-reaching reform of worship was carried out, its major consequence being the destruction and desecration of the sanctuary of Bethel and of numerous other unidentified 'high-places' where the older Canaanite religion had survived. This linking of the book of Deuteronomy with Josiah's law book provided scholarship with a firm date from which to work, lending important support to the critical contention that much, and most probably all, of the Pentateuch was only given written form in an age much later than the time of Moses.

From a literary perspective this observation offered an important insight into the history of the development of worship and its institutions in ancient Israel, especially as Deuteronomy presented as a central feature of its teaching the centralization of all worship at one sanctuary. In the light of such a basic critical yardstick, much in the character and practice of worship in Israel could now readily be defined as either pre- or post-Deuteronomic.

What thereafter seemed necessary for critical scholarship to investigate further was how much older than the actual time of Josiah the book of the law (Deuteronomy) that had then been discovered really was. Opinion among scholars tended towards the conclusion that most of Deuteronomy cannot have been written much before the time when it was discovered, and this judgment led to the rather pointless and unhelpful assessment that the book was actually a 'pious fraud', purporting to be the law of Moses, which was placed in the temple by its authors. Such a view must be wholly set aside as unworthy of serious scholarly respect. Clearly Deuteronomy sought to express an ancient law; but equally clearly it recognized in doing so that much had happened in Israel's life which had led to that law's suffering serious neglect. This is not to minimize the high probability that, in setting out the law of Moses, Deuteronomy gave a new emphasis to features which had not previously been emphasized to the same degree.

That the law book of Deuteronomy is to be linked in some fashion with the book discovered in the temple in Josiah's time as reported by 2 Kgs 22–23 has remained a cornerstone of critical biblical scholarship. Nevertheless many of the questions that arise as a consequence of such a view are still left unanswered. Foremost here, of course, must be the question whether the book had originated very much earlier and had simply been left undiscovered in the temple archives until Josiah's reform. Some views concerning the book, among them that it was a kind of 'constitution' emanating from the age of the pre-monarchic amphictyony, could be accommodated to such a claim for a very early origin. It could then be assumed that, after the introduction of the monarchy, if suffered a long period of neglect. This, however, must be looked upon as unlikely, since there is far too much in the book itself which reflects, often albeit indirectly, the era and political circumstances of the age of Josiah and even beyond it. Without wanting to prejudge important issues, there would seem to be little to be gained in supposing that Deuteronomy had enjoyed a long period as a hidden document before it became an effective instrument of Israel's policy. It is far better to accept that its authors tried hard to preserve something in Israel's life that they felt to be indispensable and ancient, rather than that they were fortunate enough to find an ancient scroll which happened to suit their needs exactly!

From what we have already noted regarding the complex literary structure of the book of Deuteronomy it is evident that we need to consider whether the original scroll covered only the original law code of Deut. 12.1–26: 15, or whether it embraced a larger part of the extant work. For a long time the former position appealed to scholarship and was embraced by many critics, even though it is a rather rough and ready assessment. We have drawn attention to the fact that in the overall structure of the book the major beginning and ending are to be found in 4.44 and 28.68, suggesting that these at one time marked the scope of its contents. However, what is likely to be misleading in drawing the conclusion that the law book was the original Deuteronomy and that the Introduction and Epilogue are simply expansions of it, is that this allows too little room for the fact that the law section in 12.1–26. 15 has also undergone expansions. We have already made much of the point that this has certainly taken place in the case of the Introduction and Epilogue. Nevertheless we have noted the primary point that it is in the law code section of the book that the earliest parts are to be found.

Deuteronomy

All of this suggests that we should exercise considerable caution in asserting a precise identification between the law book found in the temple in Josiah's time and the present book of Deuteronomy. A considerable number of scholars recognize that some connection between the two is to be upheld; at the same time few feel particularly confident in venturing to define exactly what form and length the law book displayed when it was the subject of the momentous discovery in Josiah's time. In the minds of many recent scholars, the more the character and assumptions of Josiah's reform are examined, the more oblique would appear to be the link with the book of Deuteronomy. This is not to deny that such a link existed, but only that it was probably of a rather different order from what earlier scholars had assumed to be the case. There are undoubtedly some who would view the law book as the product of Josiah's reform rather than its presupposition, and there are certain features which should point our thinking towards seeing a substantial element of truth in this conclusion. All of this shows that, before we can hope to reach a clear verdict on the question of the scope of the law book that was found in Josiah's time, we should look more closely at the nature and presuppositions of the reform that took place in that king's reign. This we can only do by means of a consideration of the broader political situation which pertained in Judah during Josiah's reign and which continued after his death.

From the point of view of the political situation in which the book of Deuteronomy emerged, a number of considerations have increasingly come to the forefront of discussion during the twentieth century. These have tended to overlay the more narrowly conceived question of the date of origin of the book of Deuteronomy, and have led to some very significant changes of emphasis.

2. The Political Background

When looked at from the point of view of what political changes lay at the back of Josiah's reform in 622 BC two features become clear. The first of these is that the presupposition for such a reform must lie in the weakening, and eventual collapse, of Assyrian control over Judah which began to take place during Josiah's reign, possibly from as early as 630 BC. For a century since the time of the Syro-Ephraimite war in 736-733 BC, when Isaiah the prophet had been active, Judah had been under the suzerain authority of Assyria. By the time that Josiah came to the throne in 639 BC as a boy of eight, the effective power of Assyria in the western parts of the empire was already greatly weakened as tension and rebellion in the east increased. This inability to assert effective control over Judah, and the accompanying lessening of any evidence of Assyrian power there, were the major factors in the politics of Josiah's reign. It cannot be regarded as unrelated to this that a great reform of religion took place in Judah according to 2 Kgs 22–23. The reform must, in much that it endeavoured to achieve, have been a resurgence of a sense of Judean independence and freedom from Assyrian control. It is scarcely thinkable that Josiah and his court did not actively strive to bring about such freedom, and to remove the last vestiges of Assyrian domination in their territory.

There is, however, a further factor that calls for reflection in gaining an understanding of the political situation out of which Deuteronomy emerged. For three centuries, since the death of Solomon, the sister kingdoms of Judah and Israel had been divided from each other. A central issue in the division had focussed upon the dynastic kingship of the house of David to which the northern kingdom had been unwilling to remain loyal. When we examine the account of the measures taken by Josiah in the fulfilling of the demands of his reform we find that central to them was the destruction of the sanctuary at Bethel and the violent suppression of its priesthood (2 Kgs 23.15-20). Clearly this can only be interpreted as a very determined attempt on Josiah's part to reunite Israel into a single kingdom, taking full advantage both of the weakness to which Assyrian control had reduced the northern territory and of the improbability of any direct Assyrian attempt to prevent his endeavours. Josiah, and the court circle which stood close to him, were ambitious of remaking a kingdom of Israel after the traditional image which they retained of the greatness that it had enjoyed in the days of David and Solomon. The themes of the oneness of Israel and of its unique and privileged destiny among the nations as a result of its divine calling could be given very bold political expression in the age of Josiah. As we have seen, these themes are certainly to be found amply expressed in Deuteronomy, but with certain cautionary refinements which suggest that it would be rash to suppose that these features of the book are simply the literary foundation for Josiah's ambitious goals.

It is in the light of this broader consideration of the political developments that were taking place in Judah during Josiah's reign (639-609 BC) that we can better understand the political significance of the teaching of Deuteronomy. The reform of worship in Jerusalem took place, according to 2 Kgs 22.3, in the eighteenth year of this king's reign (623–622 BC), and he himself was killed in battle against the Egyptians at Megiddo in 609 BC (2 Kgs 23.29-30). This latter event must be understood both as further evidence of the ambitious political expectations that Josiah nurtured for restoring Israel as a major power and as a massive setback to their fulfilment. In its own way this awareness of expectations of political greatness combined with disillusionment and disappointment in fulfilling them has an important contribution to make in enabling us to understand many of the features of the book of Deuteronomy. As we have noted, it is a law book with a highly spiritual amd moral tone, rather than a formal political charter such as we should have expected from the hands of a strong and aggressive court circle. Furthermore this markedly inward and religious tone that prevails throughout the book strongly suggests that the event of Josiah's death in 609 BC, and the further consequences that flowed from it, are also reflected in its make-up.

We have concluded from the literary form and structure of Deuteronomy that it was not composed at a single stroke as a carefully planned and unified whole, but rather was put together in stages by a process of supplementation and expansion. To begin our examination of the political background to the book with the conviction that it must be related in some way to the law book of Josiah's reform by no means resolves all the issues. We must go on to consider for how long the process of adding to Deuteronomy continued and what events may have served to stimulate these additions.

After Josiah's death in 609 BC, the dead king's son Jehoahaz (Shallum) was appointed king in his stead. After three months, however, he was removed by the Egyptian Pharaoh and replaced by his brother Eliakim (Jehoiakim) who appears to have been a more compliant vassal (2 Kgs 23.34-35). By 604 BC however, the power of Babylon had replaced that of Egypt as the controlling force in Judah's affairs.

When Jehoiakim rebelled against Babylon, Judah's resistance was quickly swept aside and Jerusalem was captured after a siege in 598 BC. By this time Jehoiakim was dead and his successor, Jehoiachim, was deported to Babylon along with many other citizens and priests from Judah (2 Kgs 24.10-17). With this there began the time of the Babylonian exile, even though a Davidic king remained on the throne of Judah for a further decade in the person of Zedekiah. After further rebellion against Babylon, Jerusalem was again besieged, captured and subsequently severely punished in 587 BC. The temple was destroyed and the last of the Davidic kings removed from office. The catastrophe of 609 BC, therefore, which and resulted in Josiah's death, was closely followed by even worse catastrophes during the next two and a half decades.

The issue for scholars of the book of Deuteronomy has been how far these later events, leading up to the destruction of the temple in 587 BC, are also to be found reflected in the literary development of the book. It is hard to present clear conclusions substantiated by firm evidence. Nevertheless it does appear that at least the first capture of Jerusalem by the Babylonians in 598 BC and the beginning of the period of the Babylonian exile have been reflected in some of the expansions to the book of Deuteronomy. The warnings of defeat, the horrors of siege and exile are all spelled out very fully in the list of curses in Deut. 28.25-68. Of course, such portrayals of disaster could have arisen on the basis of even earlier experience. Nevertheless the sharpness with which these warnings are given strongly suggests that Judah had passed through some very ruinous and trying times since Josiah had embarked upon a reunification of Israel. It is the change of tone, from one of national hope and bold expectation to one of tension, fear and solemn warning, that strongly points us to conclude that many parts of the book of Deuteronomy, especially in the Introduction and Epilogue, are sensitive to Judah's misfortunes at the hands of the Babylonians. If this is the case, then it would also appear highly probable that the major catastrophe occasioned in 587 BC, by the destruction of the royal palace and temple in Jerusalem and the downfall of the Davidic kingship, is also to be found reflected in its warnings. This viewpoint has been increasingly accepted by scholars; and the present book of Deuteronomy has been seen more as the product of Josiah's reform than as its basic presupposition.

What we have learnt concerning the political background to the reign of Josiah, and its implications for an understanding of the reform of worship throughout the kingdom in the eighteenth year of his reign, has a considerable bearing on our understanding of the book of Deuteronomy. We may note the following salient points: 1. It must be accepted that the primary aims of the reform were part of the attempt to re-establish a single unified kingdom of Israel with its religious capital in Jerusalem. At its head was to be a monarch of the dynasty of David. 2. So far as any removal of evidence of non-

Yahwistic religious traditions is concerned, this was simply part of
the larger concern to reaffirm Israel's separate identity and freedom
from external political and religious interference. A century of
Assyrian impositions and demands had been painfully felt, especially
during Manasseh's reign. 3. The extent to which the remarkably
personal and inward reinterpretation of worship and social concern
which we find in Deuteronomy formed a part of Josiah's reforming
zeal must be seriously questioned. 4. Taken together these factors
point us to recognize that it was only after the original political
ambitions of Josiah's reign had foundered with this king's death and
the arrival of the Babylonian forces in Judah that a much more
inward and spiritual concern to reform Israel's religion occurred. It is
in this sense that we can see how much that we now find in
Deuteronomy is a consequence of the disappointments that followed
on the achievements of Josiah, rather than a presupposition of them.
5. We may accept, therefore, that modern scholarship has been right
in recognizing that a connection exists between Deuteronomy and
the law book discovered in the temple in 623/2 BC in the course of
work upon the temple. It has been wrong, however, in identifying
that law book too closely with the present book of Deuteronomy.
Almost certainly the present narrative of 2 Kgs 22, with its great
emphasis upon the momentous importance of the rediscovery of the
law book, represents the work of a historian writing probably as
much as half a century after the events he describes. He was
concerned to place an emphasis of a rather different kind from that
which the original court circle of Josiah would have placed on these
events. He did so because he was writing with the benefit of the
hindsight provided by a knowledge of the events, largely ruinous in
their character, which had befallen Judah and its kings after Josiah's
untimely end.

3. The Identity of the Deuteronomists

So far we have spoken of the authors of Deuteronomy simply as 'the
Deuteronomists' without further enquiring about their identity. It is
in fact striking that, although they declare so clearly the issues for
which they stood, and the things that they would not stand for, they
do not directly reveal their own identity. As an initial attempt to
reach a conclusion on this point, it might appear to be sufficient to
note the links that must have existed between those who produced
the book of Deuteronomy and those who had stood close to king

Josiah and the work of reform. We can further note the importance in the account of the reform of such named persons as Shaphan the Secretary and Hilkiah the High Priest (2 Kgs 22.3, 4, etc.). The very warm approval expressed by the historian of 2 Kgs 22–23 of Josiah and his actions, coupled with his evident enthusiasm for the reform itself, might be thought to support the idea that the Deuteronomists were *a circle of high officials of Jerusalem* who stood very close to the king and who had been able to win him over to their cause. This has some basis of commonsense reasoning in its favour, but, on closer examination cannot be the whole truth.

Very prominent among the counter-arguments to such a position is the recognition that the Deuteronomic law of the king in Deut. 17.14–20 puts the whole case for the kingship so reticently, and with such evident caution and restraint, that it is inconceivable that it could itself be the work of a strongly pro-monarchic court circle. We have only to consider the immensely elevated role ascribed to the king in such royal psalms as Pss. 2, 45, 89, 101, 110 and 132, and to contrast this with what we find in Deuteronomy, to see how markedly guarded the Deuteronomic legislation really is. Far from seeking a strong and effective king, it looks for one who is to be a pious student of the law!

We have also had occasion to note the high probability that the exceptional degree of importance given to the work of Moses in the book of Deuteronomy arose out of a desire to offer a fundamental alternative to a powerful monarchy. This accords with the way in which Deuteronomy seeks to provide Israel with a national 'polity', or constitution, before the introduction of the kingship. Josiah's ambition to free Israel from all taint of Assyrian suzerain control after the horrors of Manasseh's reign was rather different from the aims that now appear to be uppermost in Deuteronomy. In addition to this we may note that, so far as priestly support for Josiah's reform was concerned, 2 Kgs 23.9 makes it clear that a primary contention of Deuteronomy, viz, that all levites can be priests, was not accepted by the priests of Jerusalem. It is hard to believe, then, that even if some *Jerusalem priests* supported the Deuteronomists' cause, any substantial number of them did so. That Hilkiah, the Chief Priest, did so can only be a matter of conjecture.

What we have said about the differences discernible between the central issues in the book of Deuteronomy, and what we can recognize from the nature of actual events as the primary aims of Josiah's reform, further supports such a conclusion. We may turn, then, to consider another avenue of investigation in the effort to find out more about the authors of Deuteronomy. It is notable that the book expresses a high opinion of the *prophets*, and goes so far as to present Moses himself, their great hero and example, as himself a prophet (Deut. 18.15-22). There are, besides, many indications in other writings where the influence of the Deuteronomists has been thought to be evident (see below in Chapter 7), which could point to the Deuteronomists as being a group who were deeply influenced by the prophetic circles which had flourished in Israel and Judah (so E.W. Nicholson, *Deuteronomy and Tradition*, Oxford: Blackwell, 1965, pp. 58ff.).

Attractive as such a conclusion at first appears, it is subject to such strong objections that it must be set aside. Most marked here is that, although the book speaks favourably of the prophets as a whole, the roles that it ascribes to them hardly give them a very magisterial position. They are closely linked to dream interpreters, and are only a little better than soothsayers and diviners (Deut. 18.9-22; cf. 13.1). When a fuller, and more positive, picture of the work of prophets is set out, it is wholly in terms of their task as preachers of repentance, calling Israel back to observance of the law (2 Kgs 17.13-16). This is altogether too oblique and stereotyped a picture of Israel's prophets at work to permit the conclusion that the Deuteronomists were themselves immediate disciples of the great prophets. They admittedly present Moses as a prophet, but also make it clear that he was much more than a prophet (Deut. 34.10-11). This points us in the direction of accepting that the Deuteronomists, while full of respect and admiration for the prophets as examples of a deep and passionate loyalty to Yahweh as God, and as men who had spoken up for the integrity and religious calling of Israel, were not, however, prophets themselves. They do not speak in the manner of prophets, and they consistently interpret the role of the prophets in a very distinctive way. They make them out to be educationists and national reformers, and they display almost nothing of the highly articulate prophetic speech-forms.

A further, and rather different, possibility concerning the identity of the Deuteronomists, has been strongly canvassed by M. Weinfeld (*Deuteronomy and the Deuteronomic School*, pp. 244ff.). Noting that the Deuteronomists clearly expected to be able to utilise all the administrative powers of the state in implementing their policy of maintaining a strict and rigorously enforced loyalty to Yahweh alone as God, Weinfeld further pointed to what he regarded as a number of marked affinities with the speech-forms and didactic aims of the *wisdom writers*. Believing that such wisdom skills were especially nurtured in the circles of government and state administration in ancient Israel, he argued that the circle of the Deuteronomists could most probably be found in such governmental groups. Certainly there are some points here that deserve attention, and it is undoubtedly significant that the rhetorical style that so predominates in the homilies of Deut. 5–11 suggests the experienced skills of men who were used to public speaking. The art of preaching and persuasion throbs through such speeches in an unmistakable fashion. Nonetheless the close identification of the pursuit of wisdom with a kind of ancient Israelite civil service is far from being proven. As with the claims that the Deuteronomists were to be found among disciples of the prophets, so with this claim to a wisdom connection; there are some affinities, but there are also marked differences. In spite of some links with the rhetorical flourishes of the wisdom writers, Deuteronomy is far from being a typical wisdom book. It sets out to be a law book, which would certainly presuppose some close connections with a governmental law office, but only very imperfectly adheres to a truly legal structure and style.

All of these considerations warn us against attempting to identify the Deuteronomists directly with any one professional class in ancient Israel. We can best think of a 'Reforming Party' with members drawn from more than one group of leading citizens. There would seem to be good reason for recognizing that the book of Deuteronomy was composed as a document which sought to achieve a new kind of unity in Israel. It found in the series of crises through which Judah was then passing opportunities for pressing for a deep and nation-wide 'return' to Yahweh alone as God. It believed that the lessons of the past, especially bearing in mind the terrible fate that had overtaken the Northern Kingdom in the century since Assyrian power had become dominant in the region of the Levant, called for a renewed vision of a purged and purified Israel.

4. Deuteronomy and the Northern Kingdom

One feature of the distincitive teaching of Deuteronomy has repeatedly drawn the attention of scholars during the twentieth century. This is the extent to which the book reflects the traditions, theology and political aims of the Northern Kingdom of Israel. When the ten northern tribes seceded from loyalty to the Davidic crown

after Solomon's death in 922 BC Israel became effectively divided
into two kingdoms. The Deuteronomists with their emphasis upon
the unity of Israel clearly saw in this event a major disaster. It is
clear, nonetheless, that most of the early traditions that have been
preserved for us in the Old Testament reflect a Judean (southern)
background. All too little has been preserved for us concerning the
life and religious traditions of the Northern Kingdom, save in the
rather polemically oriented accounts in the books of 1 & 2 Kings (for
example, the Elijah–Elisha stories of 1 Kgs 17–2 Kgs 9). Since much
in Deuteronomy is clearly distinctive and neither pro-monarchic nor
pro-Davidic, nor even pro-Jerusalem in an unqualified sense, may its
teaching itself not have derived ultimately from North Israelite
circles? Such was the conclusion presented in 1923 by the Scottish
Old Testament scholar A.C. Welch (*The Code of Deuteronomy. A
New Theory of its Origin*, Edinburgh: T. & T. Clark, 1923); and it is a
view that has found many supporters since then.

Welch argued that much that now appears as distinctive in
Deuteronomy—for example, its teaching on the celebration of
Passover—does so because it represents a crystallization of the
traditions of the tribes of the Northern Kingdom. Some of these may
have had very early roots, even antedating the time when the
monarchy had sought to bring together all the tribes under the
umbrella of a single nation. Such a notion of the reasons for the
apparent distinctiveness of the Deuteronomic teaching, coupled with
Deuteronomy's own claim to be ancient and authentic to the time of
the nation's beginnings, clearly have a certain appeal.

In spite of the attraction of such a position, it can certainly not be
sustained in anything like the form in which Welch presented it. As
we have seen, the consciousness that pervades all of Deuteronomy of
a major threat to Israel's political survival breathes through and
through the atmosphere of the late seventh century BC. Awareness of
the threat to Israel's land, government and social cohesion posed by
Assyrian suzerainty is far too prominent a feature of Deuteronomy to
be ignored.

G. von Rad (*Studies in Deuteronomy*, pp. 60ff.) in a major study of
certain characteristics of Deuteronomy, presented a rather different
case for a northern background to the teaching of Deuteronomy. He
saw in the book the product of a movement which had originated
with *levitical priests* who had once served at the sanctuaries of the
Northern Kingdom. These had been dispossessed of their livelihood
under the pressure of Assyrian interference when much of the

territory of the Northern Kingdom had been torn from Israel. Having fled south to Judah they found there hope for the survival and preservation of the authentic tradition of Israel which had originated with Moses. They inevitably found much in the religious life and politics of Judah which conflicted with their own points of view. At the same time they saw in the survival of this kingdom and the government of Jerusalem the only hope for the continuance of the traditions to which they were so deeply committed. They strove to warn Judah of its peril, lest the same fate overtake this kingdom as had overtaken the north, and at the same time they sought to reform the worship and life of the land to bring it into conformity with their own ideas and ideals.

In one particular respect, von Rad suggested, the northern background to Deuteronomy, which he believed to be recognizable, had a special significance. This was the regulation concerning the centralisation of worship at one single shrine. Quite evidently in the seventh century BC this must have been an allusion to Jerusalem, but it may not always have been so. He noted that Josh. 8.30ff. refers to Joshua's building an altar near Shechem 'as it is written in the book of the law of Moses', and that Jer. 7.12 refers to Shiloh as the place where Yahweh had first caused his name to dwell. From these references, as well as from certain other features concerning worship in Israel before Solomon's building of the temple, von Rad went on to suggest that at least this centralizing formula may 'in the last resort go back to one of the shrines in the kingdom of Israel (perhaps Shechem and Bethel)' (cf. G. von Rad, *Comm.*, p. 94). Undoubtedly a number of possibilities are open for consideration here, so that some deep and significant links between the book of Deuteronomy and the Northern Kingdom must be considered. The question still remains, however, whether these traditions had been given firm written form before the composition of Deuteronomy. Most of the points that have been raised in support of the contention that Deuteronomy reflects an origin in the Northern Kingdom amount to little more than indications that the book appears to have been conceived as an attempt to establish a broadly based 'compromise' polity for Israel. It incorporates elements of tradition from both Ephraim and Judah (cf. my essay 'Deuteronomy and the Jerusalem Cult Tradition', *VT* 15, 1965, pp. 300-12). How far, therefore, Deuteronomy contains authentic rules concerning patterns of worship and social administration which are drawn from the Northern Kingdon and how far it simply sets out what was felt in the late seventh century BC to be acceptable to the remnants of that kingdom after a century of Assyrian control, remains a matter for speculation. Nevertheless, with all the inevitable uncertainties, many scholars have remained of the opinion that, even if the law of cultic centralization was from the outset intended to concede certain of the claims of the powerful authorities in Jerusalem, other features of the book drew from older northern traditions.

Although von Rad's position differs substantially from that of A.C. Welch, we can see that it is not entirely unrelated to it as a hypothesis concerning the origin of Deuteronomy. A further markedly different approach regarding the book's northern origins was presented by A. Alt ('Die Heimat des Deuteronomiums', *Kleine Schriften* II, Munich, 1953, pp. 250-75). Much of Alt's contention focussed on the distinctive conceptions of kingship and political organization which he discerned in the book. It is important, then, to bear in mind that, although many scholars have embraced the general idea that much that is distinctive in Deuteronomy originated from the Northern Kingdom, there have been very wide divergences as to which features support such a claim.

There are certainly grounds for recognizing in Deuteronomy *both* remnants of the traditions and cultic conventions of the north *and* features which must be more directly related to the Jerusalem cultus. N. Lohfink has also sought to demonstrate this possibility ('Die Bundesurkunde des Königs Josias (Eine Frage an die Deuteronomiumsforschung)', *Biblica* 44, 1963, pp. 261-88, 461-98) in a rather different way; similarly M. Weinfeld (cf. 'The Emergence of the Deuteronomic Movement: The Historical Antecedents', *Das Deuteronomium*, ed. N. Lohfink, Leuven, 1985, pp. 76-98).

In discussing the claim that a very close identity can be discerned between the aims of Josiah's reform and the teaching of Deuteronomy we noted that marked differences have increasingly come to be noted. It has inevitably appeared attractive to account for these differences by the contention that the authors of Deuteronomy were not drawn from a central Jerusalem circle, either of priests or administrators, but by men who had fled from the Northern Kingdom and had resettled in Judah. Such a position must certainly command continued respect as a major possibility. At the same time, attractive as it is, we are forced to admit that it relies in part on claims that cannot properly be tested. We know too little about the differences between the religious traditions of north and south in Israel to build too much upon particular theories concerning them.

Scholarship undoubtedly passed through a phase when rather exaggerated and implausible differences were posited which could not properly be demonstrated. There are clear reasons for noting in the prophecies of Amos, Isaiah and Micah, and possibly in Hosea also, an awareness that some sense of the 'oneness' of Israel as the people of God had deep roots in the life of the nation.

It would, then, be more likely that Deuteronomy was a literary product of a movement which set great store by this notion of Israel's unity. It is this passionate concern with the nation's oneness as the people of God that stands out in the book's teaching more than any demonstrable indication that it was distinctively favourable to Ephraimite traditions. This would point us to find in Deuteronomy the expression of ideas and ideals that had at least a century of history behind them. What made the age of Josiah so important for the work of such a movement was that it provided the political opportunity when many of its goals could be realized. At first considerable success seemed promised to them, until the arrival of the Babylonians plunged Judah into an even greater time of misfortune than it had suffered during the preceding century.

Further Reading

The large number of questions relating to the historical time and political background to Deuteronomy have been the subject of extensive coverage in all the major Introductions to the Old Testament (e.g. B.S. Childs, O. Kaiser, J.A. Soggin, W.H. Schmidt and R. Rendtorff). Cf. also J. Maxwell Miller and J.H. Hayes, *A History of Ancient Israel and Judah*, London: SCM, 1986, pp. 391-402. In addition the following two essays are especially recommended: M. Weinfeld, 'The Emergence of the Deuteronomic Movement: The Historical Antecedents', *Das Deuteronomium*, ed. N. Lohfink, Leuven, 1985, pp. 76-98, and N. Lohfink, 'The Cult Reform of Josiah of Judah: 2 Kings 22-23 as a Source for the History of Israelite Religion', *Ancient Israelite Religion, Essays in Honor of Frank Moore Cross*, ed. P.D. Miller, Jr., P.D. Hanson and S. Dean McBride, Philadelphia, 1987, pp. 459-76. A slightly earlier survey article on the subject by N. Lohfink, 'Zur neueren Diskussion über 2. Kön. 22-23', is to be found in *Das Deuteronomium*, ed. N. Lohfink, Leuven, 1985, pp. 24-48.

The whole subject of the impact of Assyria upon the politics of Judah during the relevant period is extensively examined in the major work by S. Spieckermann, *Juda unter Assur in der Sargonidenzeit* (FRLANT 129; Göttingen, 1982). Cf. also M.D. Cogan, *Imperialism and Religion: Assyria, Judah and Israel in the Eighth and Seventh Centuries BCE* (SBLMS 19, Missoula, 1974).

7

DEUTERONOMY
AND THE SOCIAL
DEVELOPMENT OF ISRAEL

IN EXAMINING THE CENTRAL theological themes of the book of Deuteronomy we have already drawn attention to the fact that this book is very deeply concerned with the idea of Israel as the chosen people of Yahweh its God, and focusses particular attention on ideas of covenant and land as part of the outworking of this. There are, in reality, two focal centres around which the teaching of the book has been collected and constructed. These are the affirmation that Yahweh, the Lord God, is one, and that Israel, the uniquely chosen people of this God, are one people. We have further noted that an important step forward in Deuteronomy studies was made by G. von Rad in 1929 with his examination of the idea of the people of God in the book. This is yet further enhanced by noting the claim of S. Dean McBride (see above p. 17) that the contents of the book can best be described as constituting a 'polity' for Israel.

Undoubtedly neither the traditional understanding of 'law', as concerned directly and exclusively with legal affairs, nor that of 'instruction' as a preoccupation with individual moral and spiritual education can provide an adequate description of the contents of the book. It is more akin to a 'constitution' for a nation, embracing moral, legal, political, economic and educational issues as well as religious ones. So it has been important for the progress of scholarship that it should recognize in Deuteronomy a most important witness to the overall social and cultural development of Israel. All the more is this so in view of the fact that some of the most detailed and far-reaching attempts to define and elucidate the social and political character of this people have concentrated upon the earliest period, before the monarchy was introduced. Inevitably such studies have been contested and remain unclear because of the piecemeal and limited nature of the information that we have for such an early period. Now that we have arrived at a highly probable date for the origin of Deuteronomy in the period between Josiah's accession in 639 BC and the time of the Babylonian exile at ca. 560 BC we may be said to have a document which is much more revealing regarding the overall picture of Israel's life which can be examined to see what light it sheds upon the social development of the nation in the closing years of its existence as an independent state.

1. **The Structure of the State**

Various attempts have been made to define what is implied by the concept of 'statehood' in the Old Testament (cf. S. Talmon, 'The Biblical Idea of Statehood', *The Bible World. Essays in Honor of C.H. Gordon*, New York, 1980, pp. 239-48). We may distinguish three main features which contributed to this. The first is an awareness of a territorial framework—a land—which belongs to the entire nation. The second is a concept of sovereignty focussed in a single central government, which, in the ancient Near East, was almost universally expressed in the form of kingship. So ideas of monarchy and of statehood merged inextricably into one another (cf. Talmon, *op. cit.*, p. 239). The king was the state; and the state secured its divine foundation and blessing through the person of the king. The third ingredient of statehood is less precisely definable, but it consisted of a sense of common destiny given through a shared racial inheritance and belief in a shared historical identity. We can see how strongly these features appear in Deuteronomy, with its attention to the exodus experience and its emphasis upon the land, promised to the ancestors and now threatened by foreign aggression. Furthermore, the book displays a deep interest in a form of centralized government and a highly organized administration for worship and for legal affairs. It can even speak of all Israel as a nation of brothers.

What appear, at first acquaintance, to be merely surface interests—in pointing back to Moses, the deliverance by Yahweh's hand out of Egypt, and the promises and warnings attaching to the conquest and occupation of the land—can be seen, on closer examination, to be central elements designed to strengthen Israel's consciousness of being a nation-state. This is important in view of two lines of research and interpretation of Deuteronomy which have been put forward, but which need to be viewed with considerable caution. The first of these goes back to the early period of the twentieth century when attention was drawn to aspects of Deuteronomy which appear to be highly theoretical and impractical. Features relating to the centralising of worship, the conduct of war, the release of slaves and the wellbeing of the land all appear to be rather heavily idealised, and to have been based on theological rather than experimental reasonings. They project a hypothetical and overly theoretical way of living and conducting national affairs. Several scholars have drawn attention to this aspect of the teaching of Deuteronomy (cf. Weinfeld, p. 298). Certainly this feature is not to be denied altogether, but it can easily be exaggerated, and it must be set in the light of other, equally important, features of the book.

The second line of approach to Deuteronomy has been at rather the opposite end of the scale: to see the book as a repository of collected traditions, many of them of considerable antiquity, which originated in Northern Israel, most probably in the vicinity of Shechem (cf. above, pp. 79ff.). As a consequence, Deuteronomy has been interpreted as a kind of constitutional handbook for a particular region of Israel, which remained distinct from the central monarchic administration of Jerusalem. In such a perspective the theoretical features of the book could be accommodated, on the assumption that a truly national dimension of legislation and administration was not called for.

Certainly there is in Deuteronomy an element of pointing back to an older period of Israel's life as exemplary; and it is significant that, as we have noted, the monarchy is dealt with in an extremely cautious manner. Yet, with due allowance for such features, the overwhelming point of view which is assumed, argued for, and striven for, in Deuteronomy is that of a progressive, organized and prosperous nation-state. Israel is considered as a nation like other nations, yet unique because it has Yahweh as its God who will guard, guide and prosper its affairs, so long as the people respond loyally and sincerely to his revealed will. In this respect it can be regarded as certain that the demand for cult centralization was simply one aspect of a policy aimed at securing a unified, coherent and centrally administered state.

2. Deuteronomy and the Rise of Cities

In terms of the social development of Israel, one feature that is very prominently reflected in Deuteronomy is that the people are addressed as living in towns and cities. Israel has become a largely urban people, if not demonstrably in terms of a residential majority, at least in terms of a cultural and economic goal. The centres of prosperity, culture and administration are to be found in cities (cf. Benjamin, *Deuteronomy and City Life*). As a consequence it can be assumed that entire cities may defect from their allegiance to Yahweh (Deut. 13.12-18), that legal affairs will be dealt with in cities (Deut. 17.2, 8 etc.), and that warfare will involve the siege and conquest of cities (Deut. 20.10-18, 19-20). Significant too is the fact that cities are to be designated as places of asylum and refuge, thereby completely setting aside the earlier rite of asylum at sanctuaries (Deut. 19.1-13). The significance lies not simply in the use of cities for such specific needs, but rather in the manner in which Deuteronomy can take for granted that the city is central and fundamental to the economy, worship and moral welfare of Israel as a whole.

This perception regarding the marked extent to which Deuteronomy witnesses to the progressive urbanisation of Israel during the later years of the monarchy, and, equally significantly, the extent to which 'urban thinking' has permeated the religious and intellectual life of the nation, is very impressive. The manner in which Israel developed from a community of sheep-farming, semi-pastoral nomads who lived in tents, to a predominantly urban, highly organized, agrarian and mercantile people, is a mainstream feature of the cultural testimony of the Old Testament (cf. Frick, *The City in Ancient Israel*).

It should certainly be borne in mind, in noting this feature of Deuteronomy, that the city was one of the greatest—undoubtedly from a social perspective *the* greatest—of the inventions of ancient human communities. The subject is examined by M. Weber, *The City* (trans. and ed. by D. Martindale and G. Neuwirth, New York: Macmillan 1958, esp. pp. 121-56). By the organization of human communities into cities a vastly enhanced social, economic, administrative and religious life became possible. Since ca. 6000 BC, when cities first began to appear in the ancient Near East, until the present, the city has made possible a greater production of wealth, a more secure and readily defensible way of life, and an opportunity for cultural enrichment which could not exist without it. It is not by chance that it was from the headship of one city over a league of smaller ones that the nation-state emerged. In fact the rise of cities is inseparable from the rise of civilization itself. Nowehere in the Old Testament do we obtain a fuller and clearer picture of the commerce, administration and appeal of city life to ancient Israel than in the book of

Deuteronomy. Undoubtedly the period of history under the divided monarchy from Solomon's death until the accession of Josiah had been one of steady and impressive urbanisation. The consequences of this are brought home to us by the book of Deuteronomy. However much an older ideal of tent-dwelling tribespeople still lives on as a rather archaic image, the practical reality that Deuteronomy discloses to us is of a people who either already are town-dwellers, or may expect to become such.

3. Wealth and Poverty

The most immediate, and socially consequential, result of the process of social change that had overtaken Israel was the greater distinction that it brought between the rich and the poor. Cities created wealth. They fostered the division of labour by enabling farmers to produce a saleable surplus; they established the mechanisms for the storage of grain and for building up substantial capital holdings, and they devised systems of land purchase and the opening up of a trade in luxury goods. It needs constantly to be remembered that Israel's close neighbours, the Canaanites, and their other near neighbours, the Phoenicians, were among the foremost practitoners of international trade in the eastern Mediterranean. The consequence, inevitably, was that some people became rich, while others, through the misfortune of failed enterprises, bad harvests or poor management, became poor. All of this is well brought out in the book of Deuteronomy.

An obvious, yet very meaningful, consequence of this growth in wealth for many Israelites was the wide use of money as a means of exhange. So we find in Deuteronomy that very fundamental aspects of family life, involving protection of women in marriage which would at one time have been handled individually between the families involved, are made liable to substantial monetary fines (Deut. 22.19). Similarly a prohibition against selling a wife, who had been chosen from among captives, is laid down (Deut. 21.14). Monetary compensation is thereby shown to have become an established part of Israel's legal procedures.

However, it is most markedly in its endorsement and encouragement of the setting up of mercantile enterprise, and in the institution of capitalist finance, that Deuteronomy shows how extensively the use of money had affected Israel's life. Loans to fellow Israelites are forbidden to bear interest, although this is permitted in deals with foreigners (Deut. 23.19-20). The taking of goods in pledge requires special provisions and limitations (Deut. 26.6, 10-13), and the payment of wages to a hired labourer calls for special provisions, lest advantage be taken of a poorer citizen (Deut. 24.14-15). Deuteronomy envisages that even the tithe, one of the oldest and most sacred of the agricultural institutions by which God, the Giver of all life-enhancing crops, was honoured, could be converted into money and subsequently spent in whatever way was appropriate as a means of thanking God (Deut. 14.24-27).

That such an entrepreneurial attitude to life could bring misfortune on some is fully recognized, and special controls are introduced to try to soften the worst impact of this. Two major pieces of Deuteronomic legislation reflect this concern. The first provides for the institution of a year of release 'at the end of every seven years' (Deut. 15.1), when creditors are commanded to forgo reclaiming outstanding debts (Deut. 15.1-11). Even more significant, since it reflects a practice that had become a notable feature of Israel's life, was the legislation designed to soften the consequences of debt-slavery (Deut. 15.12-18). In early Israel, we may assume, most slaves had been obtained through their being taken as prisoners of war. In Deuteronomy, however, it is made plain that a person could sell himself, or a member of his family, into slavery for a fixed period of six years. Such a selling of oneself for slave service would normally arise through non-payment of debt, but it is also possible that the initial loan might have been taken for a wide variety of purposes. The consequences for an individual family could have been extremely damaging and destructive (cf. Amos 2.6). The Deuteronomic legislation, which in some respects appears to leave too much to the individual's conscience, discloses a surprisingly advanced and wealth—oriented community. Not surprisingly, poverty is presented as a thoroughly bad thing (cf. Deut. 15.4, which rather contrasts with the realism of 15.7). Hence it is no cause for surprise that, prominent among the blessings promised for obedience to the divine law are prosperous farm enterprises (Deut. 28.3-6, 11), with the assurance that Israelites will become creditors to other nations. Similarly the curses that are threatened for disobedience affirm menacingly that the very reverse could happen (Deut. 28.15-24, 44). All through the book of Deuteronomy we are made to recognize that Israel has developed economically to a very substantial degree and has begun to participate fully in the prosperity and trading activities that were changing the entire face of the ancient Near East.

In many respects we may argue that it is this ethos of an economically advanced community, where a substantial proportion of citizens live in houses in cities, that indicates so certainly that Deuteronomy reflects a period of national life in the late monarchy. Although, therefore, the book points back to the era of the wandering in the wilderness as a pattern period of divine leadership and guidance, it does this with a deep consciousness that such an age has passed. Israel is a nation, like other nations; and its citizens participate fully in the trading ventures of the ancient world. Money and capital have become factors which control the daily lives of most people, which enter deeply into the legislative processes of the community, and which are regarded as providing desirable goals to work for, even though they involve substantial risks.

It is in this context that a special interest attaches to the social implications of the strong Deuteronomic interest in the land as the national inheritance (cf. above, pp. 55f.). We have noted that the language that had earlier attached to land as a communal heritage of individual tribes has been transferred to describe Israel's land as a *national* heritage. Furthermore, the Deuteronomists insist that this is the case because the entire nation acquired its entitlement to the land simultaneously by right of conquest. Richly theological as such a perspective can be seen to be, emphasising its character as a divine gift, it should not be overlooked that it also served to uphold a firmly centralized administrative policy over the land. Comparative studies of the impact of monarchic administration upon societies, both ancient and modern, serve to show that control over the ownership and transfer of land was almost invariably one of the prime means by which royal authority and political control were maintained. By controlling ownership of land, kings secured power over the primary resource of food production and wealth. Alongside taxation of trading enterprises such activity provided an important basis of power for the king, enabling expensive building and military operations to take place.

4. From Charisma to Institutions

There is yet another aspect of the social development of Israel which is very revealingly shown by the book of Deuteronomy: a move in the direction of conformity and rationalisation. It may, in fact, be argued that the very idea of Deuteronomy as a book describing and defining national policy, administrative procedures and ethical goals indicates such a move. In studying the rise of governments and administrative authority M. Weber noted that 'It is the fate of charisma, whenever it comes into permanent institutions of a community, to give way to powers of tradition or of rational socialization' (*From Max Weber, Essays in Sociology*, ed. H.H. Gerth and C. Wright Mills, London; Routledge & Kegan Paul, 1948, p. 253). This process of rationalizing and institutionalizing patterns of leadership and authority in a community is well illustrated from the book of Deuteronomy. Prominent here is the setting of tests by which authoritative prophets are to be recognized (Deut. 18.15-22) and undesirable prophets rejected (Deut. 13.1-5). The most severe punishment available to the community is imposed upon offenders (13.4).

In a comparable fashion the appointment of a class of judges and officers to administer legal affairs displays a similar shift in the direction of bureaucracy and rationalization. The older pattern of priestly authority in legal matters is severely curtailed (Deut. 17.8-13). A wide range of matters involving sexual and marital behaviour is also made subject to fixed laws, whereas earlier the private judgment of priests and heads of families would have had a prominent contribution to make (cf. Deut. 22.13-30). With such written pronouncements, a substantial step has been taken in the direction of the 'routinization' of social and family life. A considered set of reasoned formulas has been established for the entire nation to obey; officials have been appointed (possibly by the central administration, although the precise basis is not specified), and large areas of life, both of the individual and the larger community, have been made subject to a carefully preserved written rule-book.

Further Reading

For the Israelite understanding of the state the best available summary of research is to be found in R. de Vaux, *Ancient Israel. Its Life and Institutions*, ET John McHugh, London: Darton, Longman & Todd, 1961, esp. pp. 91-163. For the importance of Deuteronomy as witness to the spread of urban culture in Israel cf. Frank S. Frick, *The City in Ancient Israel*, SBLDS 36, Missoula: Scholars Press, 1977 and Dom C. Benjamin, *Deuteronomy and City Life*, Lanham: Univ. Press of America, 1983. Useful material relating to wealth and poverty in the Old Testament is to be found in the survey essay by Donald E. Gowan, 'Wealth and Poverty in the Old Testament. The Case of the Widow, the Orphan and the Sojourner', *Interpretation* 41, 1987, pp. 341-53. Much relevant material is also to be found in the two books by M. Silver, *Prophets and Markets. The Political Economy of Ancient Israel*,

Boston: Kluwer-Nijhoff, 1983 and *Economic Structures of the Ancient Near East*, London: Croom Helm, 1985.

Although not directly related to the case of Deuteronomy and ancient Israel, the major studies by M. Weber that have been collected by S.N. Eisenstadt (*Max Weber on Charisma and Institution Building*, Chicago and London: University of Chicago Press, 1968) shed much light on the book.

8

DEUTERONOMY
IN THE
OLD TESTAMENT

W E HAVE ALREADY pointed out, both in connection with the distinctive style of the book of Deuteronomy and also in relation to its central theological themes, that it brings to the fore certain features of Israel's faith which have had a profound effect upon the entire Old Testament. Deuteronomy represents a kind of mid-point in the development of Israel's religious and political institutions, and, even more enduring it its effect, establishes a pattern which is then found more widely in the Old Testament. It can, with good reason, be claimed as expressive of the 'centre' of Old Testament faith. This undoubtedly means that other parts of the Old Testament are frequently examined and evaluated in the light of what has been concluded regarding the literary origin and faith of Deuteronomy.

1. The Relationship of Deuteronomy to the Structure of the Pentateuch

Deuteronomy is the fifth and last of the five books of Moses which now comprise the Pentateuch. Fittingly it is presented as a second giving of the law delivered to Israel by Moses on the eve of the entry into the land. It serves both as a reminder of the covenant that had already been made earlier on Mount Horeb (cf. Deut. 5.1-27) and also as a comprehensive constitution for the nation that was about to be established once the people of Israel had entered and conquered the land of Canaan. The commissioning of Joshua to succeed Moses and to lead the attack upon the Canaanite cities, then, provides a very suitable connecting link between Deuteronomy and the book of Joshua, which follows it in the Old Testament canon (Deut. 31.14-23; 34.9; Josh. 1.1-9).

From the point of view of the Old Testament story, therefore, there is no major break between the ending of the era of Moses, with which the Pentateuch comes to a close, and the beginning of the era of the 'Former Prophets', which commences with the book of Joshua. It is the division within the canon which has resulted in this becoming a major break, since the unfolding story of Israel's history continues with no significant pause.

There is another factor which has been of great importance to biblical scholarship which we cannot ignore. This is the fact that, although Deuteronomy marks the end of the Pentateuch, it was, from a literary point of view, certainly not the latest part of the Pentateuch to have been composed. Much of Exodus and all of Leviticus, besides parts of Numbers, were composed and incorporated into the Pentateuch after the completion of Deuteronomy.

This allows us to draw attention to an issue which remains unsolved in present-day analyses of the Pentateuch and which has a very direct bearing upon our understanding both of Deuteronomy and of the work of the Deuteronomists. In considering the form and structure of the book we noted (Chapter 2) that its authors clearly made use of historical information and legal materials which were to be found in other, and undoubtedly older, parts of the Pentateuch. This raises a number of further questions. The first of these is that raised by many scholars, whether, in addition to the composition of Deuteronomy, these same authors also made a substantial revision of the earlier Pentateuchal narratives (labelled JE in the conventional source-critical analysis). It has ususally been accepted that such a revision took place and that, especially in the account of God's revelation at Mount Sinai in Exod. 19-34, extensive changes were made. There can be no doubt that there are striking similarities between what now stands in the Exodus account of God's revelation on the holy mountain and what is said in regard to this in Deuteronomy. This is demonstrably true in regard to the Ten Commandments; and, as we have pointed out, scholars have in the past offered very different explanations of this feature.

The presence of a number of very close affinities in language and theology between the present narrative of Exod. 19-34 and some central aspects of the teaching of Deuteronomy could be explained in more than one way. In the opinion of several scholars this simply reflects the fact, which is demonstrable on other grounds, that the authors of Deuteronomy made use of older collections of law and historical narrative now preserved in the Pentateuch. Alternatively, it may have been these same authors who, alongside the composition of their own distinctive book, also revised and expanded the Pentateuchal narratives that were available to them. Probably we must be content with recognizing that the actual process of literary development cannot now be retraced with anything like certainty. Nevertheless the significant fact cannot be ignored that the book of Deuteronomy has exercised a very profound influence upon the growth and development of the Pentateuch in its entirety. Once the central themes and perspectives of the Deuteronomists had become established, they affected a wide range of activities and literary developments which are now a part of the Old Testament.

From the Christian point of view it is the element of continuity achieved through the story of how God fulfilled his promise to the patriarchs in the conquest of the land which has been seen as the Pentateuchal theme of over-riding importance. Jewish tradition, however, has consistently recognized and laid stress upon the unique status and importance of the Law, or Torah, which is contained in the Pentateuch, over against the message and story of the Prophets which follows. In a striking way, therefore, Deuteronomy manages to serve as a link between 'The Law and the Prophets' as well as between the exodus and the settlement in the land.

A further point which adds to our perception of the complex nature of the relationship between Deuteronomy and the remainder of the Old Testament is that, of all the major constituent elements of the Pentateuch, the book of Deuteronomy displays the most carefully considered rationalizing and co-ordinating approach to religion and its ritual expression. From a modern perspective it would be easy to label this the most 'advanced' and 'consistently theological' understanding of Israel's religion. It is also, in most respects, the most consistently moralised and ethicised approach to Israel's religious inheritance. We might therefore have supposed that Deuteronomy marks the culminating point of the literary and theological growth of the Pentatuech. This is not so, however: a very extensive layer of material now existing in the finished form of this great literary work has clearly been added later. The main part of this 'post-Deuteronomic' additional material which has contributed to the formation of the Pentateuch is usually described as 'The Priestly Document' (earlier often referred to as the 'Priestly Code', on the assumption that its central feature was a code of cultic legislation).

In order to account for this, scholars have been forced to conclude that the two major component strands of the Pentateuch, and in consequence the *two* most formative theological traditions of the Old Testament, are those of Deuteronomy *and* the Priestly Document. Without seeking to prejudge too many controversial and imperfectly grasped issues, we can nonetheless draw the conclusion that the shaping of the Pentateuch in its present form was largely a consequence of the bringing together of these two great traditions, each of which must have had its own literary expression, sometime early in the post-exilic age. The combined document then became the foundation for the development of Judaism in the post-exilic era, both in Judah and among the ever-growing Dispersion.

2. **Deuteronomy and the Prophets**

If the influence of the book of Deuteronomy is to be discerned quite widely in the present make-up of the Pentateuch, this is certainly also true when we consider the books of the Prophets which follow it. Here it is necessary to bear in mind that the Hebrew shape of the Old Testament canon regards the historical books of Joshua, Judges, 1 & 2 Samuel and 1 & 2 Kings as constituting The Former Prophets, and the books of prophecy which follow it as The Latter Prophets.

It is undoubtedly in the first of these two literary collections that the influence of the book of Deuteronomy is most prominent. Earlier scholars had noted how the editorial framework of the book of Judges in particular revealed to a striking degree the influence of the very firmly set doctrines of the Deuteronomists (cf. A.D.H. Mayes, *Judges*, OT Guides, Sheffield: JSOT, 1985, pp. 10ff.). Much the same can be seen to be true in regard to the way in which the reigns of individual kings are judged in the books of 1 & 2 Kings. It was the extent to which these Deuteronomic doctrines are present throughout the books of the Former Prophets that led to one of the major literary assessments regarding them. This was presented in 1944 by Martin Noth. It amounted to a claim that all six books of the Former Prophets were composed as a connected whole. Noth suggested that this can best be described as 'The Deuteronomistic History' (M. Noth, *The Deuteronomistic History*, ET JSOTSupp. 15, Sheffield: JSOT, 1981). The full ramifications of such a hypothesis have been much discussed, and modified in a number of respects by subsequent examination. Nevertheless the basic contention remains valid that the influence of the Deuteronomic movement upon the structure and leading ideas of all of these books is clearly evident. Detailed discussion of the questions that such an insight brings to the fore needs to be made with regard to each of the books separately. It is also necessary to take into account the point to which we have already drawn atention, that, in the process of composition which gave rise to the book of Deuteronomy, this wider link with the historical books which follow has also played a role. Most to the fore here is the contention, already put forward by M. Noth, that Deut. 1–3 was composed as the introduction to the entire history, and not simply to the law book of Deuteronomy. Overall, therefore, it is recognizable that the circle of authors whom we have come to describe as the Deuteronomists have exercised a very considerable influence in the shaping of the Old Testament more generally.

The question then arises almost of necessity whether a related Deuteronomistic influence is not also to be found in the editing of certain of the separate collections of prophecy. H.W. Wolff, in particular, has raised this question in regard to the book of Amos (cf. A.G. Auld, *Amos*, OTGuides, Sheffield: JSOT, 1986, pp. 30ff.). Once again there is a danger of assuming that certain ideas and themes originated with the Deuteronomists which may in reality have been older, and more widely accepted, than a labelling of them as Deuteronomic would properly justify. Nevertheless the case for seeing an influence from Deuteronomy in the editing of certain of the books of the prophets would appear to have strong support.

Undoubtedly the prophetic book where such an influence has been most widely discerned is that of Jeremiah. In this book the narratives involving the prophet's activities during the last days of Judah, before the Babylonains destroyed much of Jerusalem in 587 BC, as well as a number of prose sermon-like discourses, show much Deuteronomic influence. Nor can this be regarded as at all surprising in view of the closeness of the period of Jeremiah's activity to the time which we have postulated for the composition of Deuteronomy. The issue has become a much-discussed one in relation to the interpretation of the book of Jeremiah. It is sufficient here to note its existence and to draw attention to the way in which it points us to a recognition that the circle of Deuteronomic writers and scribes have left a very extensive legacy in the Old Testament. This undoubtedly extends beyond the boundaries of the single book of Deuteronomy and indicates their wider role in the collection and formation of a body of canonical literature. Furthermore it suggests very strongly that it was this Deuteronomic circle which has laid the foundation for the very idea of such a canonical body of writings.

Further Reading

For the varied views concerning the nature and scope of the Deuteronomic redaction of the Pentateuch cf. J.A. Soggin, *Introduction to the Old Testament*, ET J. Bowden, London: SCM, 1976, pp. 132-34. The question of the Deuteronomistic editing of Joshua–2 Kings is covered on pp. 161-64.

A very widespread discussion has arisen regarding the relationship of Deuteronomy to the book of Jeremiah. The following three essays are contained in the volume entitled *A Prophet to the Nations. Essays in Jeremiah Studies*, ed. L.G. Perdue and B.W. Kovacs, Winona Lake: Eisenbrauns, 1984: H. Cazelles 'Jeremiah and Deuteronomy', pp. 89-112; J. Philip Hyatt, 'Jeremiah and Deuteronomy', pp. 113-28; and J. Philip Hyatt, 'The Deuteronomic Edition of Jeremiah', pp. 247-68. The question of the Deuteronomic edition of Jeremiah's prophecies is also dealt with in E.W. Nicholson, *Preaching to the Exiles. A Study of the Prose Tradition in the Book of Jeremiah*, Oxford: Blackwell, 1970.

INDEXES

INDEX OF BIBLICAL REFERENCES

INDEX OF AUTHORS